THE BRIDGESTONE
100 BEST PLACES TO STAY IN IRELAND

2007 EDITION

www.bridgestoneguides.com

THE BRIDGESTONE

100 BEST
PLACES TO STAY
IN IRELAND 2007

JOHN McKENNA - SALLY McKENNA

E S T R A G O N   P R E S S

FIRST PUBLISHED IN NOVEMBER 2006

BY ESTRAGON PRESS

DURRUS

COUNTY CORK

© ESTRAGON PRESS

TEXT © JOHN & SALLY McKENNA

THE MORAL RIGHT OF THE AUTHORS HAS

BEEN ASSERTED

ISBN - 1-874076-81-2

ISBN 13 - 978-1-874076-81-0

TYPESET IN GILL ALTERNATE AND SABON TO

AN ORIGINAL DESIGN BY NICK CANN

ILLUSTRATIONS BY AOIFE WASSER

PRINTED IN SPAIN BY GRAPHYCEMS

WRITTEN BY JOHN McKENNA

CONTRIBUTING EDITORS:

EAMON BARRETT

KARYN BOOTH

ORLA BRODERICK

ELIZABETH FIELD

CLAIRE GOODWILLIE

LESLIE WILLIAMS

PUBLISHING EDITOR: SALLY McKENNA

EDITOR: JUDITH CASEY

NI CONTRIBUTOR: HARRY OWENS

EDITORIAL ASSISTANT: EVE CLANCY

WEB: FLUIDEDGE.IE

FOR:

Marco Bolasco

WITH SPECIAL THANKS TO

Des Collins, Colm Conyngham, Pat Curran,
Grainne Byrne, Julie Barrett, George Lane,
Frank McKevitt, Miguel Sancho, Hugh Stancliffe,
Connie McKenna, Sam McKenna, PJ McKenna

CONTACT THE BRIDGESTONE GUIDES:

We greatly appreciate receiving reports, e-mails and criticisms from readers, and would like to thank those who have written in the past, whose opinions are of enormous assistance to us when considering which 100 places to stay finally make it into this book.

Please write to:
Estragon Press, Durrus, County Cork

Or send an email via:

www.bridgestoneguides.com

Bridgestone is the world's largest tyre and rubber company

• Founded in Japan in 1931, it currently employs over 100,000 people in Europe, Asia and America and its products are sold in more than 150 countries. Its European plants are situated in France, Spain, Italy, Poland and Turkey.

• Bridgestone manufacture tyres for a wide variety of vehicles from passenger cars and motorcycles, trucks and buses to giant earthmovers and aircraft.

• Many new cars are fitted with Bridgestone tyres during manufacture, including Ford, Toyota, Volkswagen, Mercedes and BMW. Ferrari and Porsche are also fitted with Bridgestone performance tyres as original equipment.

• Bridgestone commercial vehicle tyres enjoy a worldwide reputation for durability and its aircraft tyres are used by more than 100 airlines.

• In Formula 1 Bridgestone supply tyres to leading teams and drivers, including Ferrari and Michael Schumacher. Technology developed in the sport has led to increased performance and safety in Bridgestone's road tyres.

• Bridgestone tyres are distributed in Ireland by Bridgestone Ireland Ltd, a subsidiary of the multinational Bridgestone Corporation. A wide range of tyres is stocked in its 70,000 square foot central warehouse and its staff provide sales, technical and delivery services all over Ireland.

• Bridgestone tyres are available from First Stop Tyre Centres and tyre dealers throughout Ireland.

FOR FURTHER INFORMATION:

BRIDGESTONE IRELAND LTD
10 Fingal Bay Business Park
Balbriggan
County Dublin

Tel: + 353 1 841 0000
Fax: + 353 1 841 5245

websites:
www.bridgestone-eu.com
www.firststop-eu.com

• This book is a celebration of the Irish vernacular. At a time when our hospitality culture is under threat from anonymous hotels, pretentious joints and chain developments, and at a time when every property 'developer' is re-inventing himself as a hotelier, the Bridgestone 100 Best is all about the native language of hospitality.

• We hunt down this vernacular everywhere we can, year after year, and we find it in little B&B's, small hotels, country houses, dinner'n'duvets. Those are the places you will find here, places whose survival against the bland and the ubiquitous is not something we can take for granted.

• Every year, more B&B's in Ireland are closing their doors, institutions who form the very backbone of the Irish vernacular of hospitality are being driven out of business by cost-cutting hotels erected under tax-break schemes. A vital part of our native culture is being eroded, on our watch, in our time.

• You can combat this erosion by supporting the places you will find in this book, places that speak the vernacular language of care, of hospitality, of a true welcome in the Irish style. Don't be misled by the alleged 4-star status of the bland and the uniform: Irish hospitality has no need of a star rating, for it is a beauty beyond classification.

John & Sally McKenna
Durrus, West Cork, October 2006

Something new

classic

chic

"WE MAKE THE MOST OF OUR FREE-DOMS BY LEARNING TO MAKE GOOD CHOICES ABOUT THE THINGS THAT MATTER, WHILE AT THE SAME TIME UNBURDENING OURSELVES FROM TOO MUCH CONCERN ABOUT THE THINGS THAT DON'T."

BARRY SCHWARTZ, THE PARADOX OF CHOICE

Making good choices about the things that matter is, fundamentally, what the Bridgestone Guides are all about. Hopefully, our travels and our researches unearth and promote those places and people who can help us to enjoy our choices whilst, at the same time, unburdening us from the very things that don't matter. We escape to great destinations in order to focus on what we want, and also to get away from what we don't want, or at least don't want too much of.

Quite often, our choices can mystify people. Hospitality, the standard line goes, increases in success as the establishment increases in grandeur: 5-star is always best. As with so many standard lines, this one is complete bunk, and it explains why there are so few 5-star places in this book. It also explains why there are so many simple places here, for we aren't looking for grandeur, per se.

We are looking for something deeper than the gloss, we are trying to make the choice that is all about the things that matter – comfort, welcome, trueness, a holistic well-being, the pleasures of food, company, relaxation, the pleasures of pleasure.

chic

Ballyvolane House, Fermoy	34
Blindgate House, Kinsale	35
Brook Lodge Inn, Macreddin	120
The Clarence, Dublin	61
Dolphin Beach, Clifden	69
The Glen, Kilbrittain	42
Iskeroon, Caherdaniel	81
Kelly's Resort Hotel, Rosslare	116
Kilgraney Country House, Bagenalstown	22
The Mustard Seed, Echo Lodge, Ballingarry	92
The Quay House, Clifden	73
Salville House, Enniscorthy	118
Shelburne Lodge, Kenmare	86
The Tannery, Dungarvan	111
Zuni, Kilkenny	87

classic

Aberdeen Lodge, Dublin	59
Anna's House, Comber	122
Ballymaloe House, Shanagarry	32
Ballynahinch Castle, Recess	65
Coxtown Manor, Laghey	55
Fortview House, Goleen	39
Killarney Park Hotel, Killarney	83
Kilmurvey House, Aran Islands	72
Longueville House, Mallow	45
Marble Hall, Dublin	62

new

Something new

• The Bridgestone 100 Best Places to Stay in Ireland is arranged **ALPHABETICALLY, BY COUNTY** so it begins with County Carlow, which is followed by County Cavan, and so on. Within the counties, the entries are once again listed alphabetically. Entries in Northern Ireland are itemised alphabetically, at the end of the book. All NI prices are quoted in sterling.

• The contents of the Bridgestone 100 Best Guides are exclusively the result of the authors' deliberations. All meals and accommodation were paid for and any offers of discounts or gifts were refused.

• Many of the places featured in this book are only open during the summer, which means that they can be closed for any given length of time between October and March.

• **PRICES:** Average prices are calculated on the basis of one night's stay for bed and breakfast. Prices are subject to change, and therefore can only represent a guideline.

• **LISTINGS:** In every entry in the book we try to list telephone number, (©) and internet details (⌐). We also request details of disabled access(&), the ability to cater for children, plus any other relevant details.

• **WEBSITES:** Where an entry has a website, we always print the address, as this is the place where you will find most up-to-date information as well as special offers. All the entries in all the Bridgestone Guides can be found on www.bridgestoneguides.com.

• **TELEPHONE NUMBERS:** Telephone numbers are listed using the international dialling code. If you are calling a number within the country, omit the international code and use the 0.

• **BRIDGESTONE PLAQUES:** Look out for our Bridgestone Plaques, displayed by many of our listed establishments.

ASHLEE LODGE

**Anne & John O'Leary
Tower, Blarney
County Cork**
✆ **+353 (0) 21-438 5346**
🖰 **www.ashleelodge.com**

That long-time appointment with the
Blarney stone will, if you are smart,
ensure that you get to sample the
delights of nearby Ashlee Lodge.

Everyone who goes to Ashlee Lodge just loves it to bits.
You get so well looked after by Anne and John in their
lovely – and much beloved – house that how could you
not love it to bits?

So, what's to love? Well, the comfort of the rooms, for a
start, and also their superb value for money, for these are
effectively hotel suites at guesthouse prices. There is the
relaxed ambience of the house, its comforting spacious-
ness, its never-care vibe that helps you chill out in ten seconds flat if you have been touring the highways and
byways and are sorely road-frazzled. There are the superb
breakfasts, a meal made as special as they can possibly
manage, with every good thing imaginable on offer, served
wih charm.

But, above all, there is the caring hospitality, the desire to
do whatever is necessary to make sure you have everything you need, everything you want, everything you
could possibly want. We don't know of anywhere else
that over-delivers on service in quite the way that Anne
and John do in Ashlee Lodge.

● **OPEN:** All year except 22 Dec-7 Jan
● **ROOMS:** 10 rooms, all en suite, made up of six executive rooms, two mini suites and two master suites
● **PRICE:** €70 for executive room, €80 for mini suite,
€120 for master suite, per person sharing

● **NOTES:** 🚇All major cards accepted. Dinner Tue-Sat,
€39. ♿access. No facilities for children.
Secure parking. Pet friendly.

● **DIRECTIONS:**
From Blarney, take the R617 for 1.5km journey to
Tower.

BALLYMAKEIGH HOUSE

Margaret Browne
Killeagh
East Cork
℡ **+353 (0) 24-95184**
🖱 **www.ballymakeighhouse.com**

Margaret Browne's much-respected farmhouse just outside Killeagh in east Cork is home to superb cooking and instinctive, homely generosity.

Margaret Browne is one of the veterans of hospitality in Ireland, a lady whose calling as guesthouse keeper, keen cook, and hospitality provider, has been going on for a long time now in the simple comfort zone of Ballymakeigh, just outside Killeagh village and up on the hill looking down on the N25 road.

Does her tenure at the hospitality coalface show? Not a bit. The enthusiasm remains as great as ever, and as focused as ever, as omnipresent in the greeting and the sharing of vital local information as it reveals itself in the precision and exactitude of the cooking at both breakfast and dinnertime. Mrs Browne is a serious cook, and her food is a splendid version of Irish vernacular cooking – quietly innovative, adorned with discreet personal flourishes that show a deep understanding of culinary culture, with a technique dedicated to delivering for the taste-buds. But the real maturity of Mrs Browne's experience is to be found in her calmness and collectedness, attributes that make her a superb hostess. She should be lecturing on the art of hospitallity, so she should.

● **OPEN:** Valentine weekend-1 Nov
● **ROOMS:** Six rooms, all en suite
● **PRICE:** B&B €60-€65 per person, single supplement charged high season only, €10

● **NOTES:** 🖻All major cards accepted. Dinner 7.30pm-8.30pm, €45. No wheelchair access.
Enclosed car park.
Children welcome, babysitting, 50% reduction for children when sharing.

● **DIRECTIONS:**
Signposted on the N25, 9.5km west of Youghal.

BALLYMALOE HOUSE

The Allen family
Shanagarry, Midleton
East Cork
℡ **+353 (0) 21-465 2531**
🖰 **www.ballymaloe.com**

You wish to save the planet? Well, start by staying at Ballymaloe, to get a lesson in how it can be done.

Every time we read new books detailing the state of the health of our food, and the health of our health, like Jonathan Harvey's *We Want Real Food*, or Michael Pollan's *The Omnivore's Dilemma*, we always think of Myrtle Allen. Why? Simply because the alarm bells these authors sound about food and agriculture and health are arguments Mrs Allen has voiced for decades, at the same time as putting an alternative into practice in her work in the legendary Ballymaloe House. Ballymaloe is all about pure food, local food, and it is all about respect for the land and its animals, for farmers and growers. It operates as the culmination of a food chain that practices extreme sustainability, and shows just how beautiful and noble that practice can be. There is nowhere like it, because its philosophy is unique – though many others now emulate Mrs Allen's creed. Staying here can sometimes feel as if you are at the very centre of the universe, because the practices of Ballymaloe are the practices we need to save the planet, and this work-as-theory shows how simply sensational a holistic experience that can be.

● **OPEN:** All year
● **ROOMS:** 34 rooms. No suites
● **PRICE:** B&B €110-€155 per person sharing. Single €135-€190

● **NOTES:** 🖩All major cards accepted. Dinner 7pm-9.30pm, €68 (buffet dinner on Sun night, 7.30pm). Recommended for vegetarians. Children welcome, cot, high chair, early dinner. Private parking.

● **DIRECTIONS:**
From Cork take N25 to exit for Whitegate R630, follow signs for R629 Cloyne. House is 3.2km beyond Cloyne.

BALLYVOLANE

Justin & Jenny Green
Castlelyons, Fermoy
North Cork
✆ **+353 (0) 25-36349**
🖱 **www.ballyvolanehouse.ie**

You can call Ballyvolane
Casa Schwarzenegger. Why?
Because everyone always
says, 'I'll be back'.

'What a fabulous stay we had at Ballyvolane! This is what we call an Irish Country home! We felt we were like family guests! We met lovely people there, all into their fishing and it was great fun! Justin and Jenny were absolutely delightful people and extremely welcoming. We'll be back there.'

We are getting used to this sort of feedback about Justin and Jenny Green's beautiful Ballyvolane. Indeed, it is Ballyvolane that today sets the critical benchmark for just what defines a stay at a grand country house. The definition is, in fact, simple: look at that first paragraph again: 'We felt we were like family guests!' If the Greens define the country house experience, it is because they define contemporary Irish hospitality. They are generous, patient, talented, and genuinely friendly. Yes, of course you have to pay to stay here, but as with all the best hospitality, the line between family guest and paying guest is agreeably vague. You truly do feel like the house is yours, but their secret is that that comfortable feeling is backed up by superlative professional service and cooking.

● **OPEN:** 1 Jan-23 Dec
● **ROOMS:** Six rooms, all en suite
● **PRICE:** B&B €95-€100 per person sharing. €35 single supplement.

● **NOTES:** 💳 Visa, Access, Amex. Dinner 8pm, €50, communal table. ♿ access. Private car park. Children welcome.
Self catering also available. Pet friendly.

● **DIRECTIONS:**
From the N8, south just after Rathcormac, take the turn to Midleton and look for the sign for the house.

BLINDGATE HOUSE

Maeve Coakley
Blindgate, Kinsale
West Cork
℡ +353 (0) 21-477 7858
🖰 **www.blindgatehouse.com**

Blindgate enjoys one of the
most precise and perfect
design aesthetics in pretty
seaside Kinsale.

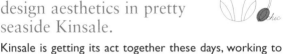

Kinsale is getting its act together these days, working to
recapture its crown back from Kenmare as the food capital of the south-west of Ireland.

A new Fishy Fishy Café is packing them in, as is the old
Fishy Fishy, Toddie's is packing them in, the new Vista is
extremely promising, and you can choose splendid places
to stay, and standards are moving up, up, up.

Blindgate House is one of the reasons why this upwards
trend is happening. When Maeve Coakley opened several
years back, she set a new benchmark for style, for service, for aesthetics, a benchmark which everyone else had
to clamber to catch up with. In this regard, Blindgate has
been an important protagonist in a town where standards had begun to slip.

Blindgate reasserted that luxury was about service and
aesthetics, and was not just about throwing money at a
place, and today it remains one of the most luxurious
places to stay, with beautiful public spaces, superb bedrooms, fantastic breakfasts, a combination of grace notes
that effortlessly make you feel like a million dollars.

● **OPEN:** Mar-Dec
● **ROOMS:** 11 rooms (seven twin rooms, three stan-
dard double rooms & one superior double)
● **PRICE:** B&B €125-€180 per room

● **NOTES:** 🖃 Visa, Mastercard, Amex. No dinner.
♿ access with assistance, but no walk-in showers.
Ample enclosed parking.
Children welcome.

● **DIRECTIONS:**
200m past St Multose Church – just up the hill from the
Kinsale Gourmet Store.

BOW HALL

Dick & Barbara Vickery
Castletownshend
West Cork
✆ **+353 (0) 28-36114**

Thirty years a-running lovely Bow Hall, and Barbara and Dick Vickery remain as youthful, as irrepressible, as vital, as hospitable, as ever.

'We still love it!', says Barbara Vickery.

Well now, isn't that just the best guarantee of a good time staying in a beautiful house that you can possibly get? After almost 30 years running handsome Bow Hall, Barbara and Dick Vickery still get that big kick out of looking after people, cooking bumper breakfasts, running a smart, sassy house that is mega-fun to stay in, in beautiful Castletownshend.

And those breakfasts! Eggs florentine with Dick's swiss chard from the garden – one guest comes back every year and eats it for breakfast every day he stays. Eggs benedict with a little splash of balsamic to cut the 'extravagant' richness of Barbara's trademark sauce. 'I just find cooking is the most wonderful outlet,' says Barbara, and boy but it shows, for Mrs Vickery has that expansive, all-encompassing American imagination when it comes to the most important meal of the day, making for some of the best breakfasts you can find. Allied to the most charming, gracious hospitality, it makes Bow Hall into the most gracious, charming place to stay.

● **OPEN:** All year, except Christmas
● **ROOMS:** Three rooms, all with private baths
● **PRICE:** €55 per person sharing,
Single supplement €5

● **NOTES:** 🖃No credit cards accepted.
Dinner, by reservation only, for special occasions only, 8pm. No ♿ access. Enclosed car park.
Children welcome.

● **DIRECTIONS:**
On the right-hand side of the road when heading down the steep hill.

KIDS WILL LOVE

1

THE G
GALWAY, Co GALWAY

2

THE GLEN
KILBRITTAIN, Co CORK

3

KELLY'S RESORT HOTEL
ROSSLARE, Co WEXFORD

4

KILLARNEY PARK HOTEL
KILLARNEY, Co KERRY

5

KILMURVEY HOUSE
INIS MOR, ARAN ISLANDS

6

KINGSFORT COUNTRY HOUSE
BALLINTOGHER, Co SLIGO

7

THE MILL
DUNFANAGHY, Co DONEGAL

8

MORRISSEY'S
DOONBEG, Co CLARE

9

PARK INN MULRANNY
MULRANNY, Co MAYO

10

RATHMULLAN HOUSE
RATHMULLAN, Co DONEGAL

CUCINA

Ursula Roncken
9 Market Street, Kinsale
County Cork
✆ **+353 (0) 21-470 0707**
⌂ **www.cucina.ie**

With smartly redecorated rooms, Ursula Roncken's pretty bed-and-bistro is always a great choice in the tourist mecca that is Kinsale.

Ursula Roncken has been working hard on the quartet of rooms for guests that sit above Cucina, her busy little town-centre bistro which has proven such a success since she opened last year.

There has been tasteful redecoration to make the rooms even smarter than before, cosier than before. We like this mix of simple rooms – you pay a flat rate for them per night and they are excellent value for money in what can be a rather pricey town – and we especially like the tasty food that Ursula and her excellent kitchen team conjure up from breakfast through to late afternoon in the bistro downstairs.

But what we like best is the striving to get better that is so evident here. Lots of tourists means that many places in Kinsale tend to just sit back and let them roll up, but Cucina is an ambitious, driven destination, with a clear and precise focus on customer satisfaction. Ursula and her crew want you to enjoy the best they can do, and this mix of simplicity, value and tasty, tasty food would find an audience in every town in Ireland.

● **OPEN:** all year, apart from two weeks at Christmas.
● **ROOMS:** Five double rooms, all en suite
● **PRICE:** €70 per person sharing, room only rate, no breakfast, though café opens early.

● **NOTES:** ▣No credit cards accepted.
Café open 8am-5pm, Mon-Sat. Breakfast served 8am-11.30pm, Lunch noon-4pm.

● **DIRECTIONS:**
In the centre of Kinsale, opposite the Kinsale Crystal shop.

FORTVIEW HOUSE

Violet Connell
Gurtyowen, Toormore
Goleen, West Cork
℘ +353 (0) 28-35324
🖰 www.fortviewhousegoleen.com

Violet Connell's B&B is the most beloved of Irish bed and breakfast addresses, and a key West Cork destination.

If you were looking for an address that defines what we mean by Irish vernacular, then Fortview can scarcely be bettered.

The welcome is true, expansive, genuinely welcoming. The design style is individual, instinctive, focused on comfort. And the breakfasts, oh my, the breakfasts! It's common to hear Violet Connell's morning feasts described as 'the best breakfast in Ireland', a mighty accolade considering the stiff competition. But... start with a compote of fresh oranges and marmalade, then proceed to Violet's own nut and grain muesli, then consider pancakes with maple syrup – that's the McKenna kids' choice – whilst the adults can't decide between potato cakes with smoked salmon, or maybe farmyard fresh eggs scrambled with chives, and all accompanied by beautiful fresh baked breads. Vernacular cooking raised to an art form, that's the Fortview breakfast, but it's also what Mrs Connell does with everything she puts her hand to in this most meticulous B&B. It's a dream destination in a dream location, a quintessential part of what makes West Cork West Cork.

- **OPEN:** 1 March-1 Nov
- **ROOMS:** Five rooms, all en suite
- **PRICE:** B&B €45-€50 per person sharing

- **NOTES:** 🖸 No credit cards accepted.
Dinner strictly by prior arrangement only, €35.
Two self-catering houses available.
No ♿ access. Enclosed car park. Children over 6 welcome in house (all ages welcome in self-catering).

- **DIRECTIONS:**
Signposted 2km from Toormore on the main Durrus road (R591). 12km from Durrus, 9km from Goleen.

GARNISH HOUSE

Con & Hansi Lucey
Western Road, Cork City
County Cork
✆ **+353 (0) 21-427 5111**
🖰 **www.garnish.ie**

Hansi Lucey's benchmark B&B is a fixture and a fitting of both the Bridgestone Guides and of Cork's hospitality scene. Long may it prosper.

Garnish House is one of the longest-established addresses in the Bridgestone 100 Best Places to Stay, earning its place since way back in 1993, when the books were in only their second year of publication.

How have things changed since then, you might ask? Well, prices have risen, of course, but otherwise Garnish remains the most constant of houses – constantly charming, constantly welcoming, constantly excellent, constantly hospitable.

Hansi Lucey seems, indeed, to have become younger over the course of the years, more capable of manning this fine big old house, still the most maternal of hostesses, fussing over all the guests, still asking if you wouldn't change your mind and have just one eclair to bring that brilliant breakfast to a conclusion. An eclair! At breakfast! Oh, all right then, just the one...

But how wonderful that amidst all the changes seen in Ireland since 1993, nothing has changed in Garnish other than that they have gotten better and better at what they do. Consistency in a world gone mad, indeed.

● **OPEN:** All year
● **ROOMS:** 14 rooms, all en suite
● **PRICE:** B&B €50-€80 per person sharing, €70-€90 single

● **NOTES:** ▣All major cards accepted. No dinner. Limited ♿ access. Enclosed car parking. Children welcome. Self-catering accommodation available with full ♿ facilities.

● **DIRECTIONS:**
Five minutes' walk from the city centre, just opposite UCC.

GLEBE SHORE

**Úna Maguire & Aveen Henry
Lisheen, Church Cross,
Skibbereen, County Cork**
℡ **+353 (0) 28-38590**
⌨ **www.glebeshore.com**

A glorious hideaway close
to the sea in West Cork,
Glebe Shore is a brilliant
new arrival on the scene.

Something new

It is a mark of the attention to detail that characterises
Aveen and Una's beautiful house that the breakfast menu
not merely lists the most mouth-watering foods you can
enjoy, but also includes a glossary of these foods.
Macroom Oatmeal is made using traditional methods in a
restored mill. Gubbeen Smokehouse is the charcuterie
business of Gubbeen farm. Glenilen Farm produces arti-
san dairy products. Staunton's puddings come from
Timoleague. Breads are sourced from Gillian Hudson's
shop in Ballydehob. Glebe is raising the bar here, showing
how care and attention can make the most important
meal of the day into a showcase for local foods. The
breakfast menu is not just a selection of good things, but
also a road map of where you are. And where are you?
Overlooking the sea in a beautifully restored house and
annex, west of Skibb, down a windy road that turns sea-
wards from the route between Clonakilty and Schull.
Glebe Shore is one of those houses that delights design
heads, whilst satisfying everyone who just wants to chill
out by being in a place that talks of its PLACE.

- **OPEN:** All year
- **ROOMS:** three rooms, all en suite
- **PRICE:** €45-€55 per person sharing, €60-€85

- **NOTES:** ▦No credit cards accepted.
Dinner available, €35.
♿ access to garden room and main part of the house.

- **DIRECTIONS:**
From N71 at Church Cross, turn left (signed Turk Head,
Lisheen, Heir Island). Travel one mile, turn left again;
after half a mile turn left again at a grassy green triangle
in the road. House is 4th entrance on the right.

THE GLEN

Diana & Guy Scott
Kilbrittain
West Cork
℡ **+353 (0) 23-49862**
🖱 **www.glencountryhouse.ie**

The Glen has become one of the great, chic, starry West Cork destinations in double-quick time.

Our friend Frank is a man of few, well-chosen words and, after he had stayed at The Glen on a trip to West Cork, we got a typically concise e-mail: 'The Glen: Superb; 3-star'.

He doesn't waste his words, does Frank, and he doesn't throw spare stars around, neither. But 'Superb' really does cover all the detail of Diana Scott's fantastic, gorgeous, covetable house. It's a place you want to stay in, and then own, a fabulous archetype of the grand West Cork manor house, close to the sea, approached through an avenue of trees, decorated with sumptuous restraint, with rolling gardens sweeping away from the front.

But 3-star? We reckon Frank means 5-star in the modern classification. The days when B&B's and country houses could only reach 3 stars, and 4- and 5-star classification was reserved for hotels, is a thing of the past. And if ever there was a 5-star West Cork house, The Glen is it.

It's a dream destination, with the most superb breakfasts, and with Mrs Scott's perky, lively energy moving everything along nicely, ever so nicely.

- ● **OPEN:** Easter-1 Nov
- ● **ROOMS:** Four rooms and one family unit
- ● **PRICE:** B&B €60-€65 per person sharing, €15 single supplement. €175 for family unit.

- ● **NOTES:** 🖃Visa Mastercard accepted.
No dinner. No ♿ access.
Secure car parking. Children welcome.
Pet friendly.

- ● **DIRECTIONS:**
Signposted from the R600, approximately half way between Clonakilty and Kinsale.

GROVE HOUSE

Katarina Runske
Colla Road, Schull
West Cork
✆ **+353 (0) 28-28067**

🖰 **www.grovehouseschull.com**

A singular style, and utterly singular
cooking, leaves some bemused by
Grove House. We love its quirkiness,
and especially its sense of difference.

Not everyone gets Grove House. The singularity of style
and service that Katarina Runske brings to this most
handsome of houses on the Colla Road, just at the top of
Schull village, can be a little disorientating for some.

Why is there a collection of shoes for sale in the front
room? Why is the menu so unpredictable – Swedish
meatballs; chicken with mustard; gravadlax; pickled her-
ring; Nico's ice creams?

But, you know, unpredictability runs in this family. For
Katarina's mum is Katherine Noren, who used to run the
legendary Dunworley Cottage, near to Butlerstown,
where she cooked food that was quite unlike anyone
else's. And now, when Katherine cooks in Grove House,
you get that same unpredictability: this cooking is distinct,
in style, in flavour, in structure. We think it is deliciously
distinct, marvellously so, and we love the bricolage nature
of the house, the style of the rooms, and the relaxed
charm of the place, and that is why Grove is in this book.
Others find the house leaves them bemused with its
conundrums, and so we must agree to differ.

● **OPEN:** all year
● **ROOMS:** Five double rooms
● **PRICE:** B&B €90-€100 per room, sharing. Single sup-
plement €50-€70

● **NOTES:** 🖎All major cards accepted. Restaurant
open daily in summer, weekends only off season. Dinner
always available for guests, €30. Private parking. No
♿ access. Children welcome.

● **DIRECTIONS:**
Take left opposite AIB, turn onto Colla Road, Grove
House is about 500 metres on the right-hand side.

KNOCKEVEN HOUSE

John & Pam Mulhaire
Rushbrooke, Cobh
County Cork
✆ **+353 (0) 21-481 1778**
🖰 **www.knockevenhouse.com**

One of the new generation of Irish hospitality addresses, Pam Mulhaire's Knockeven shows just how to run a country house with panache and style.

At a time when we read so frequently of the decline and fall of the B&B in Ireland, how splendid – and how significant – it is that talented people like Pam Mulhaire should be opening stunning new addresses for travellers such as the lovely Knockeven.

And how significant it is that Mrs Mulhaire should show, right from the outset, the key skills of cook, hostess, fount of local knowledge and all round oracle. Stay here, just on the edge of pretty Cobh, and you get the opportunity to be introduced to the culture of the entire area, thanks to a knowledgeable hostess.

Mrs Mulhaire also knows exactly how a fine period house such as Knockeven needs to be decorated in order to ensure maximum comfort. This is a sumptuous house, but everything is always pitched on the right side of restraint, nothing is showy or unnecessary, everything is informed by sheer good taste: the right object in the right place.

As you would expect, breakfasts are perfectly composed feasts of goodness, with a multitude of lovely things on the buffet and flowing freely from the kitchen.

● **OPEN:** all year, except Christmas
● **ROOMS:** Four double rooms
● **PRICE:** B&B €120 per room, person sharing. Single €75

● **NOTES:** 🖾Visa Mastercard, Laser accepted. No dinner. No ♿ access. Private parking. Children welcome.

● **DIRECTIONS:**
Leave the N25 Cork Rosslare road onto the R624, direction Cobh. Pass Fota, cross over the bridge and take the first right. At Great Island Motors turn left and it's the first avenue on the left.

CONTENTS

KILGRANEY COUNTRY HOUSE

Bryan Leech & Martin Marley
Bagenalstown
County Carlow
℡ **+353 (0) 59-977 5283**
🖰 **www.kilgraneyhouse.com**

Beautiful Kilgraney offers
one of the most total and
holistic experiences in
modern Irish hospitality.

'How do you want to feel?' is the mantra Bryan Leech
and Martin Marley have adopted for their beautiful
Victorian house, Kilgraney, and its super-funky new
Aroma Spa.

In truth, Mr Leech and Mr Marley have been answering
that question for more than a decade now, for staying and
eating in Kilgraney is such a fine experience that there is
only one way you will feel: fantastic.

They stress the holistic side of Aroma – it's not a beauty
spa, and there are no cosmetic treatments – but then
Kilgraney has always been the most holistic of places, a
destination dedicated to the aesthetics of design, good
food – particularly good food – comfort, sublime well-
being. In this sense, Kilgraney is a destination and spa
which compares to other exceptional addresses, such as
Temple Spa or Kelly's Hotel or Monart, in the sense that
well-being is paramount in everything they do, the aesthetic of the experience is total.

How do you want to feel? Blissed out? Well, in Kilgraney,
you will find that you are in the right place.

● **OPEN:** Mar-Nov, Wed-Sun
● **ROOMS:** Six double, en suite rooms & two courtyard suites
● **PRICE:** B&B €65-€120 per person sharing. Weekend
packages available.

● **NOTES:** ▭Visa, Master, Amex, Laser.
Dinner, 8pm, €48-€50, book by noon.
♿ access with assistance, please phone to discuss needs.
Aromatherapy Spa. Children over 12 only.

● **DIRECTIONS:**
Just off the R705, 6km from Bagenalstown.

22

MacNEAN TOWNHOUSE

The Maguire family
Blacklion
County Cavan
✆ **+353 (0) 71-985 3022**
🖰 **www.macneanrestaurant.com**

Neven Maguire's cooking in the MacNean has reached a new pinnacle, and the rooms are better than ever, making for an irresistible double act.

With the sort of food Neven Maguire is cooking these days – the best food of his life, and thereby some of the best food of Ireland's culinary life – you would be happy to sleep in a tent just to try the amazing tasting menu in the MacNean. But, not only has Mr Maguire climbed to a new plateau, he has also been putting his hard-earned money into refurbishing the rooms upstairs in the MacNean, working with designer Myrtle Jackson. The rooms remain simple, but they are now cosier, more comfy, with smart showers, soft colours, plump beds.

The rooms, then, define the modern Irish restaurant with rooms, or the new idea of the D'n'D, the dinner and duvet. The focus remains on the cooking, with the rooms there at keen cost in order to allow you to maximise the experience without breaking the bank. This is smart thinking, and it explains why MacNean and other D'n'D's are packed, whilst hotels and country houses with pricey rooms are empty. We all want value, and we flock to where we find it, so long as the food knocks our socks off. The cooking in the MacNean will knock your socks.

● **OPEN:** All year, except Christmas
● **ROOMS:** Ten rooms
● **PRICE:** B&B & Dinner €120 per person

● **NOTES:** 📼 Visa, Mastercard, Amex, Diners
The MacNean Restaurant opens for dinner.
No ♿ access.
Children welcomed and encouraged.
Recommended for vegetarians.

● **DIRECTIONS:**
On the main street in Blacklion, which itself is just on the border with Northern Ireland.

THE OLDE POST INN

Tara McCann & Gearoid Lynch
Cloverhill, Butler's Bridge
County Cavan
℡ **+353 (0) 47-55555**
🖰 **www.theoldepostinn.com**

The Olde Post epitomises the best of modern Irish hospitality and cooking – individual, distinct, affordable, cultured, sympathetic and creative.

The Olde Post Inn is a symbol of a culinary culture and a hospitality culture at work. Gearoid Lynch served his time in some seriously good kitchens, working alongside masters such as John Howard in Dublin's Le Coq Hardi, before decamping to his home county and to this lovely old house, just outside Butler's Bridge, to set up shop with Tara McCann, whose skills at front-of-house match those of the dynamic team at work in the kitchen.

It's a simple house, focused on comfort, focused on food, but the culture always shines through – in the cooking, which allows Mr Lynch to put his spin on several of the benchmark dishes of contemporary Irish cookery – and in the management of the house, and the concern for the guests' well-being.

To see this quietly mastered and understood culture of cooking and of hospitality at work, with its patient grace and good manners, is a vital antidote to the frenetic grasping of modern Ireland. Here are people who understand their calling, and who enact it with respect and dedication. No mean feat.

- **OPEN:** all year, except Christmas
- **ROOMS:** Seven rooms
- **PRICE:** B&B €50 per person

- **NOTES:** 💳All major cards accepted.
Full ♿ access in restaurant, but not accommodation.
Children welcome.
Dinner 6.30pm-9pm Tue-Sat; 12.30pm-3pm, 6pm-8.30pm Sun, (last orders Fri & Sat 9.30pm)€53.

- **DIRECTIONS:**
From Cavan follow N3. At Butler's bridge, take the N54 and the Olde Post is 3km further, on the right.

MORRISSEY'S

Hugh Morrissey
Doonbeg
Co Clare
℡ **+353 (0) 65-9055304**
🖰 **www.morrisseyspub.com**

A quintessential D'n'D with a rockin' restaurant, Hugh Morrissey's bar and restaurant is a star turn.

Something new

Hugh Morrissey has achieved something remarkable in Morrissey's. Long associated with good seafood cooking, the bar and restaurant used to open for only 3 months of the year. Today, this splendid D'n'D – dinner and duvet – opens for 9 months of the year and packs in ravenous food lovers, happy families, golfers and curious tourists exploring the beauties of south west County Clare. The bar has morphed into two splendid dining rooms with a small bar in the centre and a verandah looking out on the Doonbeg River. Upstairs there are seven clean, smart, lean rooms, which are as comfortable as all get out. The McKennas arrived on a Saturday night, and hoovered up seafood chowder, crab claws, sautéed prawns, Angus beef burger, fish and chips, Thai green chicken curry and ace scampi with tartare sauce, and the dining room was buzzing. The kids were game ball for sticky toffee pudding after a run around the riverbank. Then we slept the sleep of the just, had a great breakfast, and went exploring, with PJ McKenna complaining loudly that he wanted to stay another night. Who could blame him: once is not enough.

- **OPEN:** All year, except for Nov, Jan & Feb
- **ROOMS:** Seven rooms
- **PRICE:** B&B €100 per person sharing, €70 single

- **NOTES:** 📧Visa, Mastercard.
Pub restaurant opens for lunch, 12.30pm-3pm, and dinner, 6pm-9pm, €30. Children welcome.

- **DIRECTIONS:**
From Ennis, follow the Kilrush road. In Kilrush follow signs for Kilkee, and then look for the Doonbeg sign. The pub is right beside the bridge in the centre of the village.

MOY HOUSE

Antoin O'Looney (owner)
Brid O'Meara (General Manager)
Lahinch, County Clare
℡ +353 (0) 65-708 2800
🖥 www.moyhouse.com

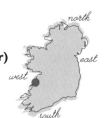

Moy House is almost dreamlike in its sublime understanding of the Irish country house experience, professionalism and personality hand-in-hand.

'Moy House was a dream,' says Elizabeth Field. touring around the banner county for a few days in August. Take it away, Elizabeth...

'I honestly think it was one of the nicest country houses I've ever been to. The room was so comfortable and tasteful, with its amazing window seats that faced the sea, its mossy-gold colour scheme, and extremely comfortable bed, pillows, sheets, lovely bathroom condiments from L'Occitane... Really beautiful breakfast, simple, restrained, light room, perfect porridge with fresh fruit and vanilla cream, good coffee, QUIET. Lively lounge for chatting in the evenings, with honour bar... we were given tea and fruitcake after coming in after a soaked walk... little bottles of Baileys in the room at night, cute alternative to chocolates.'

Well, isn't that pretty much the ticket if you are spending a few days in the banner county, getting soaked on long rambles, checking out the local music, swimming with the dolphin? Moy is magisterial in its own quiet way, and has handled recent personnel changes with comfortable ease.

● **OPEN:** Feb-Dec
● **ROOMS:** Nine rooms
● **PRICE:** B&B €170-€260 per double room, Suite €250-€295, €135-€165 single

● **NOTES:** 💳Visa, Mastercard,
Special offers Nov-May. Group rates accepted.
Dinner for residents, €50.

● **DIRECTIONS:**
Moy House is located about 1.5km south of Lahinch town, on the Miltown Malbay road. Shannon Airport is 1 hour's drive.

THE OLD GROUND HOTEL

Allen Flynn
O'Connell Street, Ennis
County Clare
✆ **+353 (0) 65-682 8127**
🖱 **www.oldgroundhotel.com**

In the centre of the town of Ennis,
and yet somehow set apart, The Old
Ground is one of the great traditional,
atmospheric hotels of Ireland.

The Old Ground Hotel is one of those few places which
are blessed with an immaculate location. It's smack in the
centre of Ennis, and indeed forms a large part of the
definition of the town.

And yet, set in its own modest grounds, it also seems
extremely private. This fabulous duality – in the centre of
everything and yet set apart – gives it a unique ambience.
Some years back, Padraig Treacy of The Killarney Park
Hotel revealed to us that when he was building the KP,
that this element of 'in the town but out of it' was just
what he wanted to achieve, and his template for doing so
was none other than The Old Ground.

Thankfully, Allen Flynn and his staff are the perfect team
to further congratulate this unique setting and ambience
with a quiet efficiency and personable style that makes
TOG all of a piece. The newest rooms on the 4th and 5th
floors are the best, we think, but wherever you find yourself in this distinguished old hotel, you feel just grand,
looked after, right at home, in the centre of the mêlée, yet
absolutely calm and collected.

● **OPEN:** Mid Jan-end Dec
● **ROOMS:** Nine rooms
● **PRICE:** €120-€200 double room,
€89-€120 single

● **NOTES:** 💳All major cards accepted.
♿ access.
The adjacent Townhall Bistro, owned by the hotel, is a
Bridgestone recommended restaurant.

● **DIRECTIONS:**
Smack in the centre of Ennis, on the corner of
O'Connell Street and Station Road.

27

STELLA MARIS

The Haugh family
Kilkee
County Clare
✆ **+353 (0) 65-905 6455**
🖱 **www.stellamarishotel.com**

A timeless sense of hospitality is the keynote of the Haugh family's little bespoke hotel, in the lively, seasidey town of Kilkee in west Clare.

The stars of the sea burn brightly along the west coast of Ireland, for whilst Ann Haugh's intimate, classic seaside town hotel does a splendid job in pretty Kilkee, this book also features the splendid Stella Maris in Ballycastle, County Mayo, another seaside beacon of good food and excellent hospitality.

Both stars are just what we go looking for in the Bridgestone Guides every year: family run addresses, where hospitality is a way of life, where care for the guest is paramount, where sustainability is a byword, where the Irish vernacular way of thinking, acting, and behaving can be seen in all its simple but resplendent glory.

Kilkee, like so many of the coastal towns in County Clare, may be changing rapidly, all too rapidly. But the Haugh family's Stella Maris changes only slowly, sustainably, successfully, and we like it like that. The design isn't cutting edge, the cooking isn't molecular gastronomy, and that's why everything feels just so right, so together, an echo of times past in time's present, things done just the way they should be, just the way they have always been.

- ● **OPEN:** All year
- ● **ROOMS:** 19 rooms, all en suite
- ● **PRICE:** €40-€75 per person sharing, single supplement for single occupancy of double room €25-€35

- ● **NOTES:** 💳Visa, Mastercard.
Children welcome.
No ♿ access to bedrooms.
Two bars, one restaurant, dinner main courses €12-€28. Private parking. Pet friendly.

- ● **DIRECTIONS:**
In the centre of Kilkee, overlooking the bay.

LONGUEVILLE HOUSE

The O'Callaghan family
Mallow
North Cork
✆ **+353 (0) 22-47156**
🖰 **www.longuevillehouse.ie**

William O'Callaghan is taking the tastes of Longueville right back to their roots, a self-sufficient cornucopia.

William O'Callaghan featured in a bumper Telegraph Magazine article in August 2006, alongside the likes of Terence Conran, Sally Clarke and Nigel Slater to name just three, where he was photographed by Toby Glanville in the midst of Longueville's 3-acre walled garden.
He has a big box of lettuces trapped between arm and hip and, despite a serious expression, he looks like a bloke who is just where he wants and needs to be.
As he gets older, William O'Callaghan goes deeper and deeper back to his roots – literally. His food is focused on his garden and his fish from the river and his game and his animals from the estate, making the food at Longueville as primal as it can get. You see this with greatest clarity at breakfast, where garden juices, garden fruits, cooked hams, field mushrooms, homemade bacon, fresh bread and a cornucopia of delicious things shout out the primacy of Longueville food in Longueville House. It is the feather in the cap of this fine big old pink house, which dates from 1820, and it means that you get the most unique tastes and treasures here in North Cork.

- **OPEN:** Mar-Dec (incl Christmas)
- **ROOMS:** 20 rooms, all en suite
- **PRICE:** B&B €235-€340 per room.

- **NOTES:** 🖃All major cards accepted. Dinner served from 6.30pm, €60. Recommended for vegetarians. Children welcome. Small weddings, themed weekend breaks (see website). Early bird 6pm-6.45pm, €40. Bar lunch available 12.30pm-5pm in bar area. Reservations advisable.

- **DIRECTIONS:**
5km west of Mallow on the N72 to Killarney.

MOSSIE'S

David & Lorna Ramshaw
Trafrask, Adrigole
Beara, West Cork
☎ +353 (0) 27-60606
🖱 www.mossiesrestaurant.com

Mossie's really is some sort of West Cork bliss, a great house, with great style, and with especially great value for money.

What a star Mossie's is. Gorgeous rooms in a gorgeous house set on a gorgeous hill overlooking Adrigole on the gorgeous Beara Peninsula. Now, that's a whole lot of gorgeous just for one place, but David and Lorna Ramshaw's country house really is someplace special.

Why it is special is no mystery. This is a particularly focused and meticulous couple, capable not merely of running a superb house with a beautiful garden, but also of smoothly running an excellent restaurant. Our last visit was a jaunt down the peninsula to try out Sunday lunch. Not only is this the best value meal in Ireland – 20euro! – it also features the ageless classics of Sunday lunch: mushroom soup, perfect roast spuds, Yorkshire pudding, roast lamb, sherry and raspberry trifle, served by super staff in the lovely dining room. The McKennas were as happy as sandboys. The bedrooms are beautifully realised, romantic and classic, especially the front room with the central bath from which you can recline in the suds whilst looking out the window and down the peninsula, glass of bubbly in hand. Some sort of West Cork bliss

- **OPEN:** All year apart from three weeks in Jan.
- **ROOMS:** Five rooms, all en suite
- **PRICE:** B&B €70-€150 per room for double occupancy, single occupancy €45-€85

- **NOTES:** 💳Visa, Mastercard accepted. Restaurant opens for Dinner, €34 and lunch on Sat-Sun, €20. Closed Mon-Wed off season.
♿ access. Pet friendly.

- **DIRECTIONS:**
12 minutes' from Glengarriff, follow the Castletownbere road, and look for signs in Adrigole.

PIER HOUSE

Ann & Pat Hegarty
Pier Road
Kinsale, West Cork
© **+353 (0) 21-477 4475**
🖰 **www.pierhousekinsale.com**

Ann Hegarty's PH is one of the great Kinsale destinations, a house that hums with the vital energy of happy, happy guests and a great hostess.

'Colourful, quirky, animated, tactile...'

Those were just some of the adjectives we scribbled in our notebook on our visit to Pier House and, we also noted, all the adjectives could apply just as well to Ann Hegarty, who runs this smashing house with a fizzing energy that is intoxicating.

Pier House really is a peach. The style is great, and it's very personal and witty. The breakfast room pulses with the energy of happy guests who have found themselves here, right smack in the centre of Kinsale, car safely parked for the night, and who can't quite believe their luck. We started receiving messages and e-mails about Pier House as soon as it opened, and the enthusiasm of travellers for passing on word of this excellent house will come as no surprise when you stay here.

Mrs Hegarty is a great host, the location is superb – albeit with a little bit of revellers' noise at busy weekends – and value for money for such comfort is terrific. One word of advice: if you only book one night at Pier House, you will regret not having booked two.

● **OPEN:** All year, except Christmas
● **ROOMS:** Nine rooms, all en suite
● **PRICE:** €120-€150 per room, including breakfast. Single €100-€140

● **NOTES:** 📼Visa, Mastercard, Laser accepted. No ♿ access. No dinner. Children welcome. One secure parking space, otherwise public carpark right next door.

● **DIRECTIONS:**
Coming from Cork, take first left at SuperValu, left at the tourist office, 50m down on right-hand side.

ROCK COTTAGE

Barbara Klotzer
Barnatonicane
Schull, West Cork
✆ **+353 (0) 28-35538**
🖱 **www.rockcottage.ie**

There is no mystery to the enduring appeal of Rock Cottage, in deepest West Cork – great cooking, great comfort, and the real West Cork vibe.

Sometimes, it is necessary to relay the entire contents of a card or a mail which we receive about one of the 100 best places to stay, simply because only then can you convey the enthusiasm of the correspondent.

Herewith the latest about Rock Cottage, Barbara Klotzer's elegant Georgian house, way, way down the Mizen Peninsula in deepest West Cork:

'My husband and I have just returned from a painting trip to Cork & Kerry – and just wanted to say how WONDERFUL was our stay at Rock Cottage. Barbara Klotzer really has produced something special there, with great attention to detail and thoughtfulness. And we have never had better dinners and breakfasts – will certainly return!'

So, thank you to Mrs A. I from Oxfordshire, who is in for a very nice surprise when she does return to West Cork and sees the newly decorated rooms that Barbara will have worked on over the winter.

Oh, and by the way, that 'wonderful' in capital letters was also underlined. Capital letters, and underlined: now that's some destination, and that's Rock Cottage.

● **OPEN:** All year
● **ROOMS:** Three en suite rooms & self-catering cottage
● **PRICE:** B&B €55-€65 per person sharing. Single supplement €25.

● **NOTES:** 💳Visa, Mastercard. Dinner, 7.30pm, book 24hrs ahead, €45, Children over 10 years welcome.

● **DIRECTIONS:**
From Schull, go west towards Goleen. At Toormore turn right onto the R591 towards Durrus. After 2.4km you will see their sign on the left.

50

SEA VIEW HOUSE HOTEL

Kathleen O'Sullivan
Ballylickey
Bantry, West Cork
☏ **+353 (0) 27-50462**
🖰 **www.seaviewhousehotel.com**

Sea View is a hotel which states and restates the enduring – and endearing – standards of great Irish hotels: conviviality, consideration, confidence.

'Roast leg of lamb, mint sauce. Roast stuffed chicken and ham. Roast sirloin of beef, horseradish sauce. Tenderloin of veal, dijon and mushroom sauce'.

Blimey, but doesn't the Sunday lunch menu in Kathleen O'Sullivan's country hotel make you nostalgic? All those dishes you thought had vanished, buried under the welter of molecular-fusion-nouvelle-whatsit that now litter restaurant menus, prove to be alive and well and flourishing in West Cork, in Sea View, in little Ballylickey.

The menu is a template for this entire hotel, a place where things are done the way they have always been done, not because they can't be bothered to change, but simply because their way is the right way. Standards mean standards here: standard dishes, high standards of service and comfort, abiding, enduring standards.

But don't think Sea View is some exercise in retro-pastiche. It isn't. It's a fine, functioning, comfortable country hotel, an archetype of its type, but it does things differently to the relentless modern zeitgeist, and that is why we respect it so much, and enjoy it so much.

- **OPEN:** mid Mar-mid Nov
- **ROOMS:** 25 rooms
- **PRICE:** B&B €130-€185 per room

- **NOTES:** 💳All major cards accepted.
Dinner in restaurant 7pm-9pm, Sun lunch (from Easter Sun) and lounge food daily. Dinner €35-€45.
♿ access.
Secure parking. Pet friendly.

- **DIRECTIONS:**
On the N71 from Cork, 5km from Bantry and 13km from Glengarriff.

REMOTE DESTINATIONS

1

DOLPHIN BEACH
CLIFDEN, Co GALWAY

2

THE G
WELLPARK, Co GALWAY

3

ISKEROON
CAHERDANIEL, Co KERRY

4

McGRORY'S
CULDAFF, Co DONEGAL

5

THE MILL
DUNFANAGHY, Co DONEGAL

6

MORRISSEY'S
DOONBEG, Co CLARE

7

MOSSIE'S
ADRIGOLE, Co CORK

8

PARK INN MULRANNY
MULRANNY, Co MAYO

9

RENVYLE
LETTERFRACK, Co GALWAY

10

STELLA MARIS
BALLYCASTLE, Co MAYO

TRAVARA LODGE

Brendan Murphy & Richard May
Courtmacsherry
West Cork
☎ **+353 (0) 23-46493**
✉ **travaralodge@eircom.net**

Brendan and Richard's
Travara is home to great
breakfasts and great craic, so
be prepared to giggle.

Readers will recall that Travara featured in the Bridgestone Guides as both restaurant and B&B for a few years, until Richard and Brendan scaled down their restaurant and took a pause to catch their breath and work out their priorities.

The reassessment led them somewhat sideways, so that their cooking is now focused on servicing the local country market and the Bandon Farmers' Market – something they have achieved with incredible success – whilst they also do some bespoke catering.

But not having the pressure of a busy restaurant has allowed them to focus more attention on their accommodation, and to max their efforts to create the most superlative breakfast for guests in their excellent, waterfront B&B in lovely Courtmac.

Add this to Richard's utterly irresistible bonhommie – Mr May is simply one of the most amusing blokes you have ever met – and Brendan's stonkingly fine cooking, and it conspires to make Travara into a dream choice in the dreamy little seaside village of Courtmacsherry.

- **OPEN:** All year, except Nov
- **ROOMS:** Six rooms, all en suite
- **PRICE:** B&B €40 per person

- **NOTES:** 💳 Visa, Mastercard, Laser
No dinner.
♿ access.
Children welcome.

- **DIRECTIONS:**
The house overlooks the bay, in the centre of the village.

CASTLE MURRAY HOUSE HOTEL

Marguerite Howley
Dunkineely, County Donegal
℡ **+353 (0) 74-973 7022**
🖰 **www.castlemurray.com**

Good flavour-filled cooking, good comfort and value, and a real Donegal welcome – that's Castlemurray.

Castle Murray House has always been the most consistent and seamless operation. Thierry Delcros ran it smoothly and reliably before passing it on to Marguerite Howley, who had herself worked alongside M. Delcros before becoming the boss.

And Ms Howley has worked with many of her crew for many years now, all of them focused on making the most of this restaurant with rooms, all of them understanding what is needed to make the customers happy, welcome, relaxed.

Mind you, even if they served gruel, you would be happy to stay in the house just to enjoy the utterly remarkable views out across the bay. Happily, the food you find in Castle Murray is always that lovely now-that's-just-what-I-felt-like! food, tasty finger-licking lobster and shellfish, fine fillets of fresh Atlantic fish treated simply and with respect, good local beef and lamb which is positively dripping with flavour. The food is another part of this seamlessly orchestrated hospitality set-up – unpretentious, honest, simple, good value, and a key Donegal address.

● **OPEN:** All year
● **ROOMS:** Ten rooms
● **PRICE:** B&B €65-€70 per person sharing. Single €80-90

● **NOTES:** 🖃Visa, Mastercard, Laser
Restaurant open 6.30pm-9.30pm Mon-Sat; 1.30pm-3.30pm, 6.30pm-8.30pm Sun; Dinner €49, Sun Lunch €27-€30
No ♿ access.
Children welcome. Pet friendly.

● **DIRECTIONS:**
Castle Murray is signposted just west of Dunkineely.

COXTOWN MANOR

Eduard Dewael
Laghey
County Donegal
☏ **+353 (0) 74-973 4575**
⌂ **www.coxtownmanor.com**

Just check out the funky,
cosmopolitan crowd you
find in Coxtown, a real
European demi-monde.

Last time we stayed in Ed Dewael's lovely country house,
we enjoyed everything – the food, the style, the service,
the lot. But what we also enjoyed was observing a won-
derfully eclectic bunch of people who were eating and
staying that night. A lively, quixotic, cosmopolitan bunch,
you found yourself wondering just where they had come
from, and just where they were going to. And how had
they had the good luck to find themselves here, just outside Laghey, close to Bridgetown, just a few miles from
Donegal town itself.

Well, by staying in Coxtown, this cosmopolitan bunch
were showing that they were well in the know, for this is
one of the best places to stay in the north west, a friendly, relaxed house that is especially winning as a place to
chill out. We have noted before that their smart Belgian-
style cooking even extends to re-making the Irish breakfast, but in truth there is a lovely confidence and fluency
in all of the food coming from the kitchen. Combined
with stylish rooms, it's no surprise that a hip European set
should choose Coxtown as their Donegal base.

● **OPEN:** mid Feb-end October
● **ROOMS:** Ten rooms
● **PRICE:** B&B and Dinner €119 wekdays and low sea-
son, €149 Sat and high season, per person

● **NOTES:** 💳 Visa, Access, Laser, Amex.
Restaurant open Tue-Sat, Dinner, 7pm-9pm.
Children welcome – family rooms.
Gourmet breaks available.

● **DIRECTIONS:**
Look for their sign on the N15 between Ballyshannon
and Donegal, turning just before the Esso station.

McGRORY'S

Anne, John & Neil McGrory
Culdaff
County Donegal
☏ **+353 (0) 74-937 9104**
🖱 **www.mcgrorys.ie**

Long celebrated as one of
the great music destinations,
McGrory's is also a smashing place to stay.

Something new

When we were first setting out to write books about
Irish food, back in 1989, Neil, John and Anne McGrory
were just assuming control of the family business, way up
north in wee Culdaff village.

Back then, McGrory's was a 10-bed guesthouse with bar
food, and it was for sale. Today, this pulsing powerhouse
of a place is pub, music venue, restaurant and comfy
rooms, and it rocks with energy and the special content-
ment of a unique destination.

Ten years after taking over, they added on the restaurant,
all the time developing the rooms, improving the offer,
polishing the offer. And, as they are musicians, they
increasingly attracted the sort of serious musicians who
appreciate being respected – the late Townes van Zandt
played here! – and the roll-call of great Irish musicians
who have plucked, fiddled and sung in McGrory's is endless. Today, Anne, John and Neil's house is a signature destination for great cooking, great craic, and great comfort.
It is also one of the most Irish of addresses, and one of
the most distinctly, distinctively Donegalese.

● **OPEN:** All year, except Christmas
● **ROOMS:** 17 rooms
● **PRICE:** B&B €50-€70 per person, €10 single
supplement

● **NOTES:** 💳Visa, Master, Laser, Amex.
Food served in bar and restaurant Mon-Sun (Oct-March
closed Mon-Tue). Restaurant Main dishes €15-€25, Bar
food €9-€15.
♿ access. Children welcome.

● **DIRECTIONS:**
On the main R238 between Moville and Malin Head.

56

THE MILL

**Derek and Susan Alcorn
Figart, Dunfanaghy
County Donegal**
☎ **+353 (0) 74-913 6985**
🖱 **www.themillrestaurant.com**

One of the many stars of
County Donegal, The Mill is
worth the lengthy pilgrimage way up north.

'Very promising', was how we described Derek and Susan
Alcorn's newly-opened The Mill, back in 2001.

Well, hand us the Oscar™ for understatement, for in just
five short years The Mill has gone from being 'very promising' to being one of the stars of Irish cooking and hospitality.

Mind you, one of the reasons why we were so understated back in 2001 was probably because Derek and Susan,
and their lovely house and its lovely restaurant, are so,
well, understated. You might attribute their lack of attention from the media to the fact that they are situated so
far north – you can't get any further north than this,
believe us – but even if they cooked in the centre of the
metropolis, this talented couple would just get on with
things. They don't make a fuss, they don't expect a fuss.
They convey their message via their work, via Mr Alcorn's
splendid Donegal cooking – this is a great destination
restaurant – via Mrs Alcorn's splendid mastery of this
most comfortable house, and all told, The Mill is promise
manifested, big time, big time.

● **OPEN:** Easter-Hallowe'en, open every night
● **ROOMS:** Six rooms
● **PRICE:** B&B €47.50 per person

● **NOTES:** 💳Visa, Mastercard, Laser, Amex.
Restaurant open Tue-Sun, dinner, €40.
No ♿ access.
Children welcome – children's menu, travel cot, babysit-
ting if needed.

● **DIRECTIONS:**
From L'kenny, take N56 through Dunfanaghy. The Mill is
1km past the village, on the right, beside the lake.

57

RATHMULLAN HOUSE

The Wheeler family
Lough Swilly, Rathmullan
County Donegal
✆ **+353 (0) 74-915 8188**
🖱 **www.rathmullanhouse.com**

Rathmullan offers one of the finest, most quintessential country house experiences you can enjoy in Ireland.

Early morning in early autumn, and there we are strolling along the shoreline, just down from Rathmullan House, working up an appetite for breakfast, working off the splendid dinner from the previous evening, recalling the brilliant creativity that is their signature – and prize-winning – scotch egg dish, the flavour-packed organic beef served with an oxtail and wild mushroom tart, then the perfect conclusion of a cocoa bean panna cotta with late-season raspberries. It doesn't get much better than that, and it doesn't get much better than this, an aura of perfect peacefulness, the Irish country house experience.

The Wheeler family have always run a special house, but the steady improvement in standards in recent years means that this is now one of the great Irish houses, a beacon of charm, hospitality, great cooking, great relaxation. Best of all, Rathmullan is one of those houses that manages to capture what is special about Donegal, whilst at the same time being itself one of the elements that makes Donegal special. It is in the culture, and it defines the culture, and that is one heck of a double act.

● **OPEN:** Open all year, apart from mid Jan-mid Feb.
● **ROOMS:** 34 rooms
● **PRICE:** €90-€140 per person + 10% service charge.

● **NOTES:** ▭All major cards accepted. ♿ access.
Swimming pool.
Rates available for longer stays, and mid-week and weekend in low season.

● **DIRECTIONS:**
From Rathmullan, left at Mace store, follow the road past the Catholic Church, then past big black gates. Rathmullan House is at the end of this avenue.

ABERDEEN LODGE

Pat Halpin
53-55 Park Avenue, Ballsbridge
Dublin 4
✆ **+353 (0) 1-283 8155**
🖰 **www.halpinsprivatehotels.com**

Aberdeen Lodge defines the
very best of Irish hospitality.
Pat Halpin should be
Minister for Tourism.

Whenever they establish task forces on tourism, how come smart guys like Pat Halpin never seem to feature on them? Of course, Mr Halpin may very well be so busy running his superb houses that he wouldn't have time to advise government ministers, or write up reports destined for dusty shelves. But, in fact, his work on a task force need only consist of having all the other guys on the force to stay for a couple of nights in Aberdeen Lodge.
That way, they could see that if Mr Halpin doesn't really talk it – he is extremely self-effacing – well then he sure as hell walks it. Aberdeen Lodge is hospitality as a textbook exercise. It is staff motivation in a style that would make management guru, Tom Peters, weep. The way Aberdeen Lodge is run is a template for every hospitality business in the country – dedicated, efficient, stylish, confident, successful, proudly Irish. Every guest who stays here feels like the cat who got the cream. This is hospitality as a sumptuous experience, an unmissable experience; this is hospitality defined. Mr Halpin doesn't need to write the report: he runs it.

● **OPEN:** All year
● **ROOMS:** 17 rooms, including two suites
● **PRICE:** €65-€90 per person sharing, €99-€120 single

● **NOTES:** 🖾All major cards accepted. Light 'drawing room' menu, €8-€15 per course, extensive wine list. Secure parking. ♿ access.
Children – not suitable for children under 7yrs.

● **DIRECTIONS:**
Just down from the Sydney Parade DART station.
Park Avenue runs parallel with Merrion Road & Strand Road.

BEWLEY'S BALLSBRIDGE

Carol Burke (General Manager)
Merrion Road, Ballsbridge
Dublin 4
✆ **+353 (0) 1-668 1111**
🖱 **www.bewleyshotels.com**

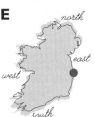

Location, value for money, and the enduring attraction of O'Connell's restaurant in the basement makes Bewley's a real shoo-in.

There are other Bewley's hotels in and around Dublin, all offering the same mixture of keen prices and good service. So, how come we choose the Ballsbridge destination alone?

Well, for a start, it's the most handsome building of them all, a lovely slice of artful Victoriana. Secondly, it is close to the city, and all you have to do is hop on a bus, or even walk down and take the DART, to be right smack in the middle of things, and you can leave the car in their underground car park. This means that for a family travelling up to town for a show or a match, you can get everyone to anywhere with minimum fuss.

But BB has a secret weapon, in the shape of O'Connell's restaurant, and O'Connell's is not just one of the favourite restaurants of the McKenna children, it is also home to Tom O'Connell, one of the restaurateurs that the McKenna parents most admire. Tirelessly inventive, and utterly self-critical, Mr O'Connell is a true star, and he runs a true star restaurant. With value for money in O'Connell's easily the equal of the value in BB, it's all ace.

- **OPEN:** All year, except Christmas
- **ROOMS:** 304 rooms
- **PRICE:** €109 per room

- **NOTES:** 💳All major cards accepted.
♿ access. Children welcome – large basement drawing room downstairs.
O'Connell's restaurant, dinner from €28.50.
Secure parking.

- **DIRECTIONS:**
On the corner of the Merrion Road, and Simmonscourt Road, adjacent to the Four Seasons Hotel and the RDS.

THE CLARENCE

Oliver Sevestre
6-8 Wellington Quay
Dublin 2
☎ **+353 (0) 1-407 0800**
🖱 **www.theclarence.ie**

The chicest of city hotels remains the chicest of city hotels, and the Tea Room is right back on top form.

With Fred Cordonnier taking the food in the Tea Rooms back to its glory days, the circle is complete in The Clarence, meaning that sublime rooms and great food are back in harmony in this iconic Dublin destination.

We have remarked before that time has not merely been kind to the design of The Clarence, but has in fact served to emphasise and underline just what a contemporary classic this entire hotel is in terms of style.

Back before Guggi fetched high prices for his pot paintings, they used them throughout the hotel, setting trends rather than simply following them.

The furniture by Lutyens is peachy, the bedroom furniture as timelessly stylish as that of the public rooms. It's an hotel that makes you feel extremely special, which, of course, it should do, given the high prices. But it does do just that, everytime you find yourself back in the big smoke, and with Dublin proving to be such a chaotic city these days, the cool international charm of The Clarence is just what you need at the end of a busy day at the coalface.

● **OPEN:** All year
● **ROOMS:** 49 rooms, incl penthouse & suites
● **PRICE:** €340-€750 per room, penthouse €2,500, excluding breakfast.

● **NOTES:** 🖃All major credit cards accepted. Lunch from €35, Dinner from €60. ♿ access. Valet parking. Children welcome.

● **DIRECTIONS:**
Overlooking the River Liffey, on the South side, approximately 150 metres up from the Ha'penny Bridge. 30-45 minutes' drive from Dublin airport.

MARBLE HALL

Shelagh Conway
81 Marlborough Road
Donnybrook, Dublin 4
© **+353 (0) 1-497 7350**
🖱 **www.marblehall.net**

With only three rooms, it isn't always easy to get into Marble Hall. Keep trying, 'cause boy is it worth it.

Last time we stayed in Shelagh Conway's Georgian house in Donnybrook, we were up in town for a big do. You know the set up – black tie, speeches, big dinner, vacuous presenters, after dinners acts you can't hear because the AV is dodgy, that sort of craic. It was great fun.

But, it wasn't as much fun as staying in Marble Hall, the house that is the best kept secret in Dublin. Now, here is a star turn, a real celeb, a class act. Marble Hall is so good you would travel to Dublin just to stay here. Never mind the big do. Forget the black tie. It's not just a bed for the night: it's a true destination, a place of fascination.

What fascinates? The polish of everything. The gleam of everything. The superlative breakfast. The sheer comfort of the room. The pleasure of being in a beautifully maintained Georgian house, between Donnybrook and Ranelagh.

After a night in Marble Hall, you feel refreshed, recharged, and even that hangover isn't a bother. That's the potency of this place – it gives you a true sense of well-being, and for us it is one of the defining addresses of the city.

● **OPEN:** All year
● **ROOMS:** Three rooms
● **PRICE:** B&B €50 per person sharing

● **NOTES:** 🖭No cards accepted.
Not suitable for children. No dinner.
Secure parking.

● **DIRECTIONS:**
Marlborough Road runs between Ranelagh and Donnybrook villages. Marble Hall is on the right-hand side, near the top of the road, driving from Donnybrook.

MERRION HALL

Pat Halpin
54-56 Merrion Road
Ballsbridge, Dublin 4
© **+353 (0) 1-668 1426**
🖰 **www.halpinsprivatehotels.com**

Merrion Hall is a genuinely
distinguished destination, a
place set apart by the enduring excellence of its service.

Like its sister address, Aberdeen Lodge, Merrion Hall
works because it has the very best staff you can find. The
next time someone tells you that young people today are
lazy, slothful and impolite, just bring them to meet the
youthful crews who work these two townhouses, and let
them eat their words.

Of course, great service requires great motivation, and it
is thanks to Ann and Pat that the sense of enthusiasm,
pride and pleasure in their work is so manifest in the
staff. Great management arrives from the top and, as
many great hospitality providers have pointed out, there
is no such thing as bad staff, only bad management.

In Merrion Hall, you see great management and great staff
in that most synergistic of relationships, one feeding off
the energy and achievement of the other.

It all adds up to the most personable, comfortable, when-
can-we-come-back? place to stay in the city. Merrion Hall
and Aberdeen Lodge truly earn the epithet 'distinguished',
for they are places of high standing, places that demon-
strate a quality of excellence, day in, day out.

● **OPEN:** All year
● **ROOMS:** 28 rooms, including eight suites
● **PRICE:** €65-€90 per person sharing, €99-€120 single,
suite supplement €50

● **NOTES:** 🖾All major cards accepted. Light 'drawing
room' menu, €8-€15 per course, extensive wine list.
Secure parking. ♿ access.
Not suitable for children under 7 years old.

● **DIRECTIONS:**
Ballsbridge is located south of the city centre and
Merrion Hall is just opposite the Four Seasons Hotel.

THE MORRISON

Sandra Doyle
Ormond Quay
Dublin 1
✆ **+353 (0) 1-887 2400**
🖰 **www.morrisonhotel.ie**

If you want to feel right at the heart of Dublin city, then The Morrison just has to be your riverside base. Step out the door, and the city awaits.

They have been busy in The Morrison, opening their art gallery and courtyard garden, developing conference facilities, polishing up their spa in advance of its opening in 2007, remaking the restaurant and bars and adding a rake of new rooms. Seven years after opening, it's good to see such a statement of faith in their future.

But, the delight is always in the detail, and three of their new innovations seem especially apt for the McKenna family. Firstly: GHD hair straighteners, for Connie McKenna, (13). Secondly, iPod docking stations, for Sam (11) and PJ (8) McKenna. Thirdly Apple Mac computers, for Sally and John McKenna (mature for their age).

Actually, all these gizmos, despite being essential for modern city life, aren't the real USP of The Morrison. That USP is the brilliant riverside location, and also the great style and comfort of the rooms. You get the real buzz and energy of Dublin city when staying here, the sense that you are at the heart of everything that is desirable about the capital city. So, hair straightened, iPods charged and work done, let's all go check out the Dublin nightlife.

● **OPEN:** All year, except 25-26 Dec
● **ROOMS:** 138 rooms, studio rooms and suites
● **PRICE:** From €340 per room. Supplements apply for suites and superior rooms.

● **NOTES:** 🖾All major cards accepted. Halo Restaurant and Cafe Bar open daily. Wellbeing Spa to open in 2007. Conference space, art gallery and courtyard garden. ♿ access. Children welcome. Parking rate offered in Jervis St Car Park.

● **DIRECTIONS:**
On the north side of the river, near the Millennium Bridge.

BALLYNAHINCH CASTLE

Patrick O'Flaherty
Ballinafad, Recess, Connemara
County Galway
℅ **+353 (0) 95-31006**
🖱 **www.ballynahinch-castle.com**

Ever seen Connemara in the snow? It's a magical winter wonderland, best enjoyed at beautiful Ballynahinch.

Our last visit to Ballynahinch coincided with a rare fall of snow in Connemara. 'The quintessential winter wonderland' we noted, proof that this magical castle can bewitch your soul even as your teeth chatter and your toes threaten to fall off. Just then a large black otter walked across the path ahead of us, straight from Central Casting. We waited for the White Witch, but she must have been filming somewhere else.

Ah, Ballynahinch. Black otters scuttling on snowy white boreens that go winding through the woods. Panache of scallop, sole and brill with a chive and smoked salmon sauce for the dinner's main course. The dining room at breakfast overlooking the river as you enjoy perfect scrambled eggs with potato cake and bacon. The leather sofa plump and inviting in front of the entrance hall fire as it blazes away. What Patrick O'Flaherty and his team do here is quite simple: they stop time, in order that you get off the real, mad, dizzying world. Ballynahinch is not of this world. It exists in another, gentler, more real, timescape. No one has told them about the 21st century. Ssshhh.

● **OPEN:** All year, except Feb
● **ROOMS:** 40 rooms, including three suites
● **PRICE:** €105-€200 per person sharing, single supplement €30

● **NOTES:** 💳All major cards accepted.
Dinner in restaurant, €55. Limited ♿ access.
Children welcome. 3-4 day breaks, special rates incl. dinner, see website for more details.

● **DIRECTIONS:**
From Galway, take signs for Clifden (N59). At Recess you will begin to see their signs.

DEVON DELL

Berna Kelly
47 Devon Park
Lower Salthill, Galway city
℅ **+353 (0) 91-528306**
🖱 **www.devondell.com**

A classic B&B in every way, Berna Kelly's great house is modest in size, but massive in generosity of spirit, of time, of patient care and attention.

Here's a funny story. A lady makes a reservation to stay with a friend at Devon Dell, Berna Kelly's modest, and immodestly wonderful B&B just outside Galway city. Turning into the small cul-de-sac where the house is, the lady decides that she isn't staying there: it simply isn't grand enough. But her friend insists that she will stay, as they had made a reservation. One stays. One goes into town and stays at one of the many bland hotels in Galway. And that is how someone who judges a book by the cover is the biggest fool of all.

Yes, Devon Dell is modest. But it is modest because Mrs Kelly's focus is on the perfection of her offer – a perfect breakfast (one of the very best). The most perfectly crisp, clean sheets on your bed. The most meticulously maintained house. The most profound welcome. The maximum assistance whatever it might be that you need, or feel you need. Berna is there to do it for you, switching the oven on at 5.30am to begin the breads and start preparing the freesh fruits and the cereals, as you slumber in dreamland upstairs. So, don't be a fool: only enter.

● **OPEN:** Feb-Oct
● **ROOMS:** 2 double rooms, twin & 1 single, en suite
● **PRICE:** €45-€50 per person sharing

● **NOTES:** 🖃No credit cards. No ♿ access.
No facilities for very young children.
Street parking just outside.

● **DIRECTIONS:**
Find Fr Griffin Rd, and follow to T-junction, where you take left into Lr Salthill Rd. After approx 500m, having passed two pubs, take first right. Go 100m to fork in road, take left and very sharp left into cul-de-sac.

DELPHI LODGE

Peter Mantle
Leenane, Connemara
County Galway
✆ **+353 (0) 95-42222**
🖰 **www.delphilodge.ie**

Delphi Lodge offers one of the classic country house experiences, touching every base between sportiness, culinary arts and primordial archetype.

We often discuss how many of the most successful addresses in the Bridgestone guides work because they offer archetypes that our subconscious desires.

Well, how many of your primordial desires are stirred by what Delphi Lodge offers? An early 19th century house built by the Marquis of Sligo, in a remote valley in mystical Connemara, surrounded by the region's tallest mountains, abutting onto a lake, with all the rooms having a view of water or hills.

A great big communal dining table, decked with silver and candlelight, with sumptuous cooking from Cliodna Prendergast, clever country cooking with modern signatures. The lively, sporty chat of new friends, everyone dressed in their best.

Sitting fireside reading a book whilst the drizzle drizzles outside, snug in the comfort of the Big House, having already selected a good bottle to go with dinner tonight. Delphi is the country house experience as scripted by J.K. Rowling, and worthy of analysis by Jung himself. As archetypes go, Delphi Lodge goes further than any other.

● **OPEN:** Mid Jan-mid Dec
● **ROOMS:** 12 rooms, all en suite (seven with lake view)
● **PRICE:** €100 per person. Upgrade to lake view room €30. Single supplement €30

● **NOTES:** Visa & Mastercard. Dinner at 8pm, communal table €50. Limited ♿ access. Secure parking. Not suitable for young children.

● **DIRECTIONS:**
1km northwest of Leenane on the Louisburgh road. In woods on left about half mile after the Mountain Spa.

DOLPHIN BEACH

Sinead & Clodagh Foyle
Lower Sky Road, Clifden
Connemara, County Galway
℗ **+353 (0) 95-21204**
🖑 **www.dolphinbeachhouse.com**

Sinead and Clodagh Foyle
define the pinnacle of Irish
hospitality and cooking in
the fab Dolphin Beach.

'This is the best kind of Irish hospitality you can find:
quirky, welcoming, innovative, professional. A memory to
savour and a place to return to.'

That was the verdict of Patsey Murphy, of *The Irish Times*,
after a couple of nights at Sinead and Clodagh Foyle's
house, on Clifden's Sky Road. Now, when you squeeze all
those adulatory adjectives into a pair of sentences, it's
going to seem a bit rich to say that Ms Murphy only does
scant justice to the experience that is Dolphin Beach.
Sorry Patsey. But it ain't enough.

Dolphin is not just the 'best kind of Irish hospitality'. It is,
we would argue, Irish hospitality defined. This is hospitality as bred in the bone. This is style as equal to any other.
This is cooking that defines Irish vernacular cuisine. And
this is a house where the welcome – unfussy, true, solici-
tous, generous – means that you are swept up into a
maelstrom of new friends, late night drinks and discus-
sions, the passion of great hospitality. All we can say about
Sinead Foyle's brilliant cooking is that you simply must try
it, and you must – must – stay at Dolphin Beach.

● **OPEN:** All year, except Christmas & New Year
● **ROOMS:** Nine rooms, all en suite
● **PRICE:** €65-€85 per person sharing.
Single supplement €20

● **NOTES:** 💳Visa, Mastercard, Laser. Dinner 7.30pm,
€37. Enclosed parking. Children over 12 welcome.
♿ access. Day trips organised.

● **DIRECTIONS:**
Take the Sky road out of Clifden, take the lower fork
for 2km. It's the house on the sea side. Clifden is
approximately 1 hour's drive from Galway.

COASTAL GETAWAYS

1
DOLPHIN BEACH
CLIFDEN, Co GALWAY

2
GLEBE SHORE
SKIBBEREEN, Co CORK

3
GHAN HOUSE
CARLINGFORD, Co LOUTH

4
KELLY'S RESORT HOTEL
ROSSLARE, Co WEXFORD

5
KILMURVEY HOUSE
KILMURVEY BAY, ARAN ISLANDS

6
McGRORY'S
CULDAFF, Co DONEGAL

7
PARK INN MULRANNY
MULRANNY, Co MAYO

8
RENVYLE
LETTERFRACK, Co GALWAY

9
STELLA MARIS
BALLYCASTLE, Co MAYO

10
TRAVARA LODGE
COURTMACSHERRY, Co CORK

THE G

Mary McKeon
Wellpark, Galway
Co Galway
☏ **+353 (0) 91-865 200**
🖰 **www.theghotel.ie**

G for Galway? G for glam?
G for gay? Actually, in 2006
G stands for gaustering.
What's your G opinion?

Something new

No other place has been so much discussed, debated, dis-agreed over and disseminated as The G. Everyone has an opinion on the Philip Treacy interior. The location. The entrance. The food. The rooms. People who haven't ben to Galway since 1986 have an opinion on the Camilla mir-rors and the Warhol chairs and the McMurray rug and the Tom Dixon lights.

So, let's try to make some thing clear. The location is bad: opposite a dual carriageway, between a cinema and a fur-niture store. And, the location doesn't matter. The G is an ocean liner: you board, and then you pay no attention to the sea all around you. Secondly, the bedrooms are maybe the best we have ever come across, and represent a new benchmark of comfort and style, with a soft and curving design that is utterly winning.

The public rooms work precisely because they are so brash and ballsy. If they had compromised an iota on the glam and the gayness, then the compromise would have been fatal. Some will love them – we do – many will hate them, but Galway has needed the G. The G is a blast.

- ● **OPEN:** All year, except Christmas
- ● **ROOMS:** 110 rooms, including suites
- ● **PRICE:** B&B €220-€450 per room

- ● **NOTES:** 🖵All major credit cards accepted. ♿ access. Valet car parking. Children welcome. Spa open 9am-9pm. Special rates + Spa treatments available, see website for more details.

- ● **DIRECTIONS:** The G is part of a shopping and cinema complex, on your right-hand side as you drive into Galway on the Dublin road, opposite Lough Atalia at the end of the N6.

THE HERON'S REST

**Sorcha Molloy
16a Longwalk, Spanish Arch
Galway, Co Galway**
℡ **+353 (0) 86-337 9343**
🖰 **www.theheronsrest.com**

Sorcha Molloy is the hostess
with the bestest breakfast. A
skilled baker with a fount of
Galway info.

Sorcha Molloy is as fine an hostess as you will meet in the
West. Her house is a smashing B&B, overlooking the
Corrib River just down from Spanish Arch. You look out
your bedroom window to see the folk feeding the swans
across the river on the slipway. On the right day you
might see Mike Lynskey, 'The King of the Corrib', launch-
ing his fine blue boat. The feeling of being right, smack,
bang in the heart of Galway is intense, but so is the feeling that you have just stumbled on a jewel-like secret.
Heron's Rest is the sort of place you feel like keeping a
secret all to yourself. But... we are generous souls at
Bridgestone Central, and we know you want the very
best, so here it is.
Ms Molloy has an instinct for hospitality, coupled with an
energy and openness that is bewitching. What she does,
she does the best – lovely rooms, beautifully arranged
flowers, robes and flip-flops to pad to your bathroom.
And breakfast is amazing – muffins with cinnamon and
pear; bread baked in her Mum's Aga; breakfast quesadilla
with poached egg; fab apricot buttermilk pancakes. Ace.

● **OPEN:** May 1-Sept 30
● **ROOMS:** Two ensuite rooms, one double, one triple
● **PRICE:** B&B €55 per person sharing

● **NOTES:** ▦All major credit cards accepted.
No ♿ access.
Street parking in front of house
Children welcome, 30% discount, camp bed

● **DIRECTIONS:** Follow signs for East Galway and
Docks. Turn left at Sheridan's on the Docks and follow
the road around to the right. Heron's Rest is facing the
water.

THE HOUSE HOTEL

Deirdre Sands
Lwr Merchant Rd, Spanish Parade
Galway, CoGalway
✆ **+353 (0) 91-538900**
🖱 **www.theHousehotel.ie**

A groovy new element of the regeneration of Galway's docklands, The House is smartly conceived, with acres of style.

Something new

The docklands area of Galway is beginning its own renaissance. Cursed with an enormous car park facing the water for most of the zone, and with handsome coal dumps and oil yards elsewhere, the area has been a useless zone for years, and has always felt as if the city has somehow decided to turn its back on the waterfront.

But now, with Sheridan's on the Docks providing a focus, with Heron's Rest B&B around the corner facing the water, with the new museum open just in front of the ever-popular Nimmo's restaurant, some energy is crawling back into this unjustly negleected area. Expect it to take off in the next few years, and expect the handsome House Hotel to be eternally packed.

The makeover of the former Brennan's Yard hotel has made The House much more visible, with its bright plumage in the reception, bar and restaurant forming a focus as you walk around from the docks. We like the sleeping cat signs, the stylish rooms, the fact that the public areas are a great place to meet up. Most of all we like the cosiness that makes the House a home from home.

● **OPEN:** All year
● **ROOMS:** 40 rooms and suites
● **PRICE:** from €220 per room, €330 per suite

● **NOTES:** 🖃All major credit cards accepted.
♿ access.
Complimentary free parking.
Children welcome. Dinner plus B&B rates available.

● **DIRECTIONS:**
Entering Galway, follow signs for city centre and docks. The House hotel is just around the corner from Sheridan's on the Docks.

KILMURVEY HOUSE

Treasa & Bertie Joyce
Kilmurvey Bay, Inis Mor
Aran Islands, County Galway
℗ +353 (0) 99-61218
accommodationaranislands.com

The best dining room of the year? Kilmurvey House takes the prize for great food and mighty, mighty fun.

The most fun dining room of all our travels in 2006? You might reckon we would plump for some big, buzzy, sexy blast of people in one of the city hotspots. Or maybe the newest boutique dining experience. Well, actually the most fun dining room of 2006 was Treasa Joyce's, in her B&B, Kilmurvey House, on Inis Mor, the largest of the three Aran Islands. It was also the wildest – those pensioners from Dublin! what juice are those guys on?! - the most cosmopolitan – Germans, Dutch, Irish, Americans, Italians, all breaking bread together – and amongst the most quixotic – those Americans are filing for divorce the moment they get back home, right?

Mrs Joyce has a fabulous team to serve her fabulous cooking, and when a huge bowl of organic salad leaves is plonked on the table followed by a starter of barley risotto in pastry cases with roasted tomatoes and basil, then the well-being level in Kilmurvey just goes stratospheric. Roast loin of pork was perfection, wild salmon with beurre blanc and tomato concassé one of the dishes of the year, and the breads are a meal in themselves. Fab.

- ● **OPEN:** 1 Apr-16 Oct
- ● **ROOMS:** 12 rooms, all en suite (seven family rooms)
- ● **PRICE:** €45-€50 per person sharing. Single €60

- ● **NOTES:** Dinner €30, 7pm, please book in advance.
No wheelchair access.
Children welcome.

- ● **DIRECTIONS:**
Take boat from Rosaveel in Connemara. When you arrive in Kilronan, the house is a further 7km from the ferry port. On arrival, take one of the tour buses that crowd down at the port.

THE QUAY HOUSE

Paddy & Julia Foyle
Beach Road, Clifden
Connemara, County Galway
℡ **+353 (0) 95-21369**
🖱 **www.thequayhouse.com**

Glorious in every detail, Paddy and Julia Foyle's legendary house is dream made reality on the waterfront.

Like the rest of us, Paddy Foyle isn't getting any younger. The difference between the rest of us and Mr Foyle, however, is that with Paddy Foyle you can never tell. The passage of time glides past him, and with his wife Julia – also seemingly oblivious to the passing of the years – he runs the mighty Quay House with panache, youth, and an almost juvenile vigour.

We have been writing about Quay House for so long that it's easy to overlook the most basic things about it. So, let's restate them: this house is one of the design glories of Irish hospitality and tourism. Each of the 14 rooms is designed differently, and each is a peach. The location – down on the quay at Clifden – is only mighty. The style of the public rooms is so gracious and provocative that you would give your eye teeth to be able to pull together something like this. Breakfasts in the conservatory are amongst the finest you can enjoy. And, finally, Mr and Mrs Foyle are amongst the truly great hosts.

Sure, why wouldn't they be, when they have obviously discovered the secret of eternal youth.

● **OPEN:** Mid Mar-Early-Nov.
● **ROOMS:** 14 en suite rooms, including rooms with kitchens
● **PRICE:** B&B from €75 per person sharing, €100-€120 single rate

● **NOTES:** 🖃 Visa, Mastercard, Laser. No dinner. ♿ access. Street parking. Children welcomed.

● **DIRECTIONS:**
Take the N59 from Galway to Clifden. The Quay House is down on the quays, past the small playground, and overlooking the harbour.

RENVYLE

**Ronnie Counihan
Renvyle, Connemara
County Galway**
© +353 (0) 95-43511
www.renvyle.com

Renvyle is a true Connemara classic, thanks to the cooking of chef Tim O'Sullivan and the hospitality of manager Ronnie Counihan and his crew.

'This was great. The best part (for now). I had lots of fun playing snooker with Dad, playing golf with Dad, going on the boat rides and rowing and going in da pool.'

Out of the mouths of babes, or ten-year-old boys like Sam McKenna anyhow, come the simple truths of a great place to stay, untarnished by his father's dubious (at best) talents with a snooker cue or a golf club. But then, McKenna Jnr. is just part of the latest generation to fall under the spell that Ronnie Counihan and chef Tim O'Sullivan weave in the laid-back benignity of Renvyle. Eating. Golfing. Boating and, above all, chilling out, is what Renvyle is all about. Indeed, this may be the most relaxed place in the entire country. The relaxed vibe induces the most spirited ambience in the dining room at dinner time, when the place erupts like one big party. And this party is driven largely by Tim O'Sullivan's superb cooking. Mr O'Sullivan has the skill to make everything wanton with taste, dripping with flavour, sheer succulent eating whether you are having guinea fowl with sausage meat stuffing or john dory with star anise beurre blanc. Great.

● **OPEN:** Feb-Dec
● **ROOMS:** 68 rooms
● **PRICE:** B&B €40-€120 per person sharing. Single supplement €20.50. Look out for offers on web-site.

● **NOTES:** All major cards accepted. Restaurant, serving dinner 7pm-9.30pm, €45. Children welcome, many facilities incl. seasonal outdoor heated swimming pool and golf course. Full ♿ access.

● **DIRECTIONS:**
The hotel is signposted from Kylemore. At Letterfrack, turn right, and travel 6.5km to hotel gates.

ROSLEAGUE MANOR

Mark Foyle
Letterfrack, Connemara
County Galway
✆ +353 (0) 95-41101
🖰 www.rosleague.com

Everyone's dream destination for a romantic west coast wedding, Rosleague is picture postcard perfect, and pitch perfect, both together.

Rosleague is dreamily perfect. A fine manorial house that sits high on the hill overlooking Ballynakill Harbour, with views out to Diamond Hill, Letter Hill and Speckled Hill, this pretty pink Regency house is magical, with every element seemingly arranged just so, for your pleasure. Small wonder, then, that it is the hottest destination for bespoke weddings in the west, for anyone who visualises their perfect day as a dream-like scenario where everything must be picture-postcard perfect is likely to see it all the more clearly when they see themselves and friends and family cavorting in Rosleague. The perfect day.

Making things perfect is the preserve of Mark Foyle, and despite his youth, this charming man has all the capabilities in the world of hospitality that has always characterised the members of the Foyle family. What we like is that everything in Rosleague is of a piece; the food, the wines – a great list – the ambience, the style, the comfort, the service, the value. So don't think you need a wedding invitation to be at Rosleague: it is one of the finest houses in the west, pretty, pink, kind of perfect.

● **OPEN:** Mar-Nov
● **ROOMS:** 16 bedrooms, four suites
● **PRICE:** €85-€125 per person sharing. Single supplement €35.

● **NOTES:** ▥All major cards accepted. Restaurant, serving dinner 7pm-9pm, €45. Children welcome. No ♿ access. Rates for dinner + B&B, and off season mid-week rates available on-line.

● **DIRECTIONS:**
Letterfrack is 11km north west of Clifden. Follow the N59. The house overlooks Ballinakill Bay.

SEA MIST HOUSE

Sheila Griffin
Clifden, Connemara
County Galway
✆ **+353 (0) 95-21441**
🖰 **www.seamisthouse.com**

A singular house, with a
singular aesthetic, Sea Mist
is in just the right place to
enjoy Connemara.

The best B&B's make the right choices for you. They put
the right furnishings in the right place. They cook the right
things for breakfast. They have all the local knowledge you
need. They are in the right place in the right place. And,
then, to cap it all, they have something a little transcen-
dent to offer also – an atmosphere, an aesthetic, a code
of being, a way of behaving, that makes you sink with
relaxation from the moment you walk in the door.

So it is with Sheila Griffin's lovely Sea Mist. It's beautifully
– and simply – designed. The breakfasts are really ace,
with lots of excellent local things to enjoy. Mrs Griffin
knows pretty much everything about everything in town
and roundabouts. The house is just down from the centre
of busy Clifden, so it's never noisy.

And, then, there is the spirit of Sea Mist, a little bit
bohemian, a little bit left-field, a little bit unorthodox, that
is the icing on the cake of a special place. The house is –
quietly, shyly – different, and we really like and enjoy that
bit. Mind you, we like and enjoy all the other bits as well.
And so will you. Trust us: you will, you will.

● **OPEN:** All year, except Christmas and midweek Nov-
Feb
● **ROOMS:** Four rooms, all en suite
● **PRICE:** €35-€55 per person sharing, single
supplement €15-€25

● **NOTES:** 🖃Visa, Mastercard, Laser. No dinner. No
♿ access. No facilities for children. Limited enclosed
parking.

● **DIRECTIONS:**
Beside the Bank of Ireland, centre of Clifden, veer left
from the square, and it's the stone house on the right.

THE CAPTAIN'S HOUSE

Jim & Mary Milhench
The Mall, Dingle
County Kerry
✆ **+353 (0) 66-915 1531**
🖱 **www.captainsdingle.com**

The Captain's is a staple of Dingle, and has been a staple of the Bridgestones for years. Stay a day or so and you'll quickly understand why.

The Captain's House has been a staple of the Bridgestone Guides for many years now. As much has changed in Dingle – including, goodness gracious, its name, so we should be talking about An Daingean – little has changed in Jim and Mary's house.

They have simply gotten better, of course, more polished, more practised, more on top of their game. But what has not changed here is the expression of hospitality in the purest, most instinctual way.

We have seen Mrs Milhench at work, for instance, and it amazes us that she can do quite so many things all at the same time. Cooking, baking, preparing, sorting, house-keeping, greeting, informing, all at the same time. Maybe it's a Kerry thing – you will find the same thing in The Park Hotel, or The Killarney Park, for instance – but it is both a joy to behold, and a joy to be on the receiving end of such amazing skill.

And that skilful hospitality means that the Captain's House is always a peachy place to stay, so cosy, so convenient, with such fabulous cooking and baking to enjoy.

- **OPEN:** 15 Mar-15 Nov
- **ROOMS:** Eight rooms, one suite, all en suite
- **PRICE:** €50-€55 per person sharing. Single rate €60. Suite €130 per room

- **NOTES:** 💳Visa, Mastercard, Laser. No meals. No ♿ access.
No facilities for children.

- **DIRECTIONS:**
Follow signs to Dingle town centre. The Captain's House is 200m on the left, after the first big roundabout.

EMLAGH HOUSE

Marion & Grainne Kavanagh
Dingle
County Kerry
✆ **+353 (0) 66-915 2345**
🖱 **www.emlaghhouse.com**

Emlagh is an oasis of cultured calm just on the outskirts of frothy Dingle, a place where Marion and Grainne strive to make everything the best.

In Emlagh House, Marion and Grainne Kavanagh's standards are such that everything is not simply the best, everything is the best it can possibly be.

The duvets are the best, the plushest. The crockery is the best, so tactile. The tea strainers – yep, the tea strainers– are the best. The power showers are the best, and indeed these are awesomely powerful, so prepare to be blasted out of your lazy Dingle hangover. The CD players in the rooms are superlative Bose, and they even have a stash of CDs you can choose from.

Being simply the best continues everywhere. Breakfast offers superb treats such as baked eggs with ham and cream and a little light cheese topping, and meantime you have to work hard to drag your gaze away from the glorious views out across the sea. The paintings and etchings they hang by Kerry painters are glorious, and whilst the house is indeed rather grand, it never feels indulgent or precious. Instead, it feels like someplace special, a house where the evident luxury is put to service to make you feel good. Simply the best, and simply the best it can be.

● **OPEN:** 10 Mar-1 Nov
● **ROOMS:** 10 rooms
● **PRICE:** B&B €90-€140 per person sharing, €40 single supplement

● **NOTES:** 📧Visa, Access, Mastercard, Amex, Laser.
No dinner.
One room fully ♿ accessible.
Private car park. No facilities for children under 8 years.

● **DIRECTIONS:**
As one drives west towards Dingle, Emlagh House is the first turn left at the entrance to the town.

HAWTHORN HOUSE

Noel & Mary O'Brien
Shelbourne Street, Kenmare
County Kerry
✆ **+353 (0) 64-41035**
🖱 **www.hawthornhousekenmare.com**

The diplomacy of hospitality is what Mary and Noel O'Brien put into practice in their B&B, Hawthorn House, smack in the centre of lively Kenmare.

A correspondent wrote to us last year and, in the course of an effusive letter praising Hawthorn House, concluded by saying that 'The O'Briens are excellent ambassadors for Ireland'.

And, indeed, Mary and Noel O'Brien are just that. Their hospitality in pretty Hawthorn, their 'warm welcome & excellently appointed bedrooms, not to mention good breakfast' is the very best kind of ambassadorial behaviour. Their work shows a quiet, calm, confident culture of hospitality at work. They do things their way, and that is a naturally Irish way, with no pretentions, no airs and graces, just quiet style, good cheer, and a fundamental concern that guests should be happy and be well minded, and be minded to return because they have been well looked after. The proof of their success, of course, is that any time you return to Hawthorn House for another blast of Kenmare's culinary energy, you recognise so many other faces, for everyone here is a regular. That is how to run a B&B and it is also, for our money, how to run a country. True ambassadors, indeed.

- **OPEN:** All year, except Christmas
- **ROOMS:** Eight rooms, en suite
- **PRICE:** €40-€45 per person sharing, Single €60

- **NOTES:** 💳 Visa, Mastercard. No dinner.
No ♿ access.
Enclosed private parking.
Children welcome, babysitting available.

- **DIRECTIONS:**
There are three main streets in Kenmare. Hawthorn House is situated on Shelbourne Street, the quietest of the three.

ISKEROON

Geraldine Burkitt & David Hare
Bunavalla, Caherdaniel
County Kerry
✆ **+353 (0) 66-947 5119**
🖰 **www.iskeroon.com**

So fabulously unreal it belongs in a comic book or a fairy tale, Iskeroon is the ultimate cult address in Ireland.

Geraldine and David Hare's otherworldly Iskeroon is, perhaps, the ultimate cult address in Ireland. It's got all the cult characteristics, all the archetypal attributes.

The location, to begin, is utterly comic-book crazy: turn off the Ring of Kerry, take all the turns down a steep hill which descends at a giddy plummet, then drive across a small beach – you always wanted to drive across a beach to get to where you are going. And then, there it is, looking out over Derrynane harbour, all but invisible from the land: real adventurers, we guess, would arrive here by yacht, powered by sail.

The design of the house, which dates from 1936, seems almost improvised, and indeed it was built without an architect. Geraldine and David complete this special template with a demon eye for detail: Iskeroon is splendidly finished in William Morris colours, with fabrics from Mallorca, and Mediterranean pottery. Above all, Iskeroon doesn't feel like anywhere else: it feels organic, both in its siting, and in its design and colours which are beautiful, and appositely chosen. It's unique, it's the ultimate cult.

● **OPEN:** 1 May-30 Sep
● **ROOMS:** Three rooms, each with private bathroom. Self-catering apartment for two
● **PRICE:** from €150 per room. Single occupancy price on request

● **NOTES:** 💳Visa, Mastercard, Laser. No meals available. No wheelchairs. No facilities for children.

● **DIRECTIONS:**
Find the Scarriff Inn between Waterville and Caherdaniel. Take sign to Bunavalla Pier. At the pier, go through gate marked 'private road', beside beach through pillars.

GREAT BATHROOMS

1
THE CLARENCE
DUBLIN, Co DUBLIN

2
EMLAGH HOUSE
DINGLE, Co KERRY

3
THE G
GALWAY, Co GALWAY

4
KNOCKEVEN HOUSE
COBH, Co CORK

5
LONGUEVILLE HOUSE
MALLOW, Co CORK

6
MONART
ENNISCORTHY, Co WEXFORD

7
MOSSIE'S
ADRIGOLE, Co CORK

8
MOY HOUSE
LAHINCH, Co CLARE

9
THE OLD CONVENT
CLOGHEEN, Co WATERFORD

10
THE ROSS
KILLARNEY, Co KERRY

THE KILLARNEY PARK HOTEL

Padraig & Janet Treacy
Kenmare Place, Killarney
County Kerry
℃ **+353 (0) 64-35555**
🖰 **www.killarneyparkhotel.ie**

Benchmark standards in
every department make
choosing the Killarney Park
the simplest of choices.

It has become the fashion nowadays, in an age of showy wealth, to fly to New York to do some Xmas shopping.
So, just before last Xmas, we went to Killarney, to get away from all the clamour about shopping in New York. And, do you know what, we now reckon a pre-Xmas break is just what you need to survive the clamour of the festive season. A few days in the Killarney Park, this most benchmark of hotels, is just the job for chilling out and steeling yourself for the, ahem, fun to come. And no air-port queues. No customs. No excess baggage.
So, we had a lovely time, enjoyed the lovely cooking of Odran Lucey, enjoyed the market in town, tried a spot of ice skating – with faltering grace – and enjoyed the food in the bar – the best bar food in Ireland, bar none. We swam in the pool, we strolled around the town. We had a ball. Then we drove home, recharged, reinvigorated.
So, for Xmas 2006, and Xmas 2007, the choice is simple. Mind you, the stellar standards of the KP make it a simple choice at any time of the year. A truly great hotel is for always, we reckon, not just for Xmas.

● **OPEN:** All year, except Christmas
● **ROOMS:** 68 rooms
● **PRICE:** €270-€400 per room, €375-€760 suites

● **NOTES:** 💳Visa, Mastercard, Amex, Laser. Restaurant & Bar, Dinner €60. Children welcome, babysitting and facilities available on request. ♿ access.
Spa open 10am-8pm

● **DIRECTIONS:**
At 1st roundabout in Killarney (coming from Cork), take 1st exit for town centre. At 2nd roundabout take 2nd exit and at 3rd roundabout take 1st exit.

THE PARK HOTEL

Francis & John Brennan
Kenmare
County Kerry
℮ **+353 (0) 64-41200**
🖰 **www.parkkenmare.com**

Their Samas spa is state-of-the-art, but it is the practice of hotel-keeping as an art form that remains the USP of Kenmare's wondrous Park Hotel.

We had a lunchtime meeting with a friend in the Park Hotel during the year. Coffee in the bar, a chat, that sort of thing.

As we arrived, Francis Brennan was acting as major-domo in the reception area. He was, as ever, in his element. We have never – never – seen a human being dispense information, gossip, advice, instruction, enquiry, concern, and sympathy, to so many people in such a short space of time. He was there, at the centre of things, doing what a great hotelier does – he was acting as the heartbeat of this great hotel.

In the lounge, the coffee and cakes was nothing less than a feast. Meticulously served, gargantuan in extent, this was coffee and cakes for the gods.

So, we know a great deal of attention has been paid to Samas, the hotel's awesome spa. But don't overlook the thing that Francis and John Brennan have been doing for decades. It is called hospitality, the art of hotel keeping, and it is conducted here with a passion and skill that makes us think of Toscanini working an orchestra.

● **OPEN:** 18 Apr-30 Nov & 23 Dec-2 Jan. Weekends only in Nov
● **ROOMS:** 46 rooms
● **PRICE:** B&B €166-€228 per person sharing. Suites & de luxe rooms €317-€385. Single €206-€256

● **NOTES:** 💳 All major cards accepted.
Restaurant open daily, Dinner from 7pm, €69. ♿ access. Secure parking. Luxury spa. Children under 4 years sharing, complimentary.

● **DIRECTIONS:**
At the top of Kenmare town.

THE ROSS

Padraig & Janet Treacy
Town Centre, Killarney
Co Kerry
☏ **+353 (0) 64-31855**
🖱 **www.theross.ie**

north

east

west

south

Something new

The hottest new address in Killarney is actually one of the town's oldest establishments, The Ross.

Padraig and Janet Treacy are amongst the finest hoteliers in Ireland, achieving standards in The Killarney Park that are positively stratospheric. But long before they opened the KP, it was in the family's hotel, The Ross, that Mr Treacy cut his teeth. 'I worked the tables there, and I love it, because that's where I was born', Mr Treacy explained to us once.

That affection is evident in every inch of the reborn The Ross. This 30-bed boutique is a beaut: glamorous, colourful, fun, vivid, funky, sharp, sensual. Every room has a glimpse from the windows of the lovely St Mary's Cathedral, a peach of a Gothic Revival church, and the contrast between its aged magnificence and the cutting-edge style of the bedrooms in The Ross is a fabulous juxtaposition, and shows the smartness of the reconstruction that such an element was considered so important. The public rooms and Cellar One restaurant are done out in Warholian electric colours, vivid limes and pinks and cool blues, and once again the Treacys have raised the benchmark in Killarney for style and service. Truly hot.

● **OPEN:** All year
● **ROOMS:** 29 rooms and suites
● **PRICE:** B&B €170-€225 per room, €220-€275 per suite, €130 single

● **NOTES:** 💳All major credit cards accepted. Cellar One Restaurant open for breakfast, lunch & dinner. ♿ access. Private car parking. Children welcome. Leisure facilities of the Killarney Park available to guests.

● **DIRECTIONS:**
In the centre of Killarney, just round the corner from the main high street, beside the church.

SHELBURNE LODGE

Tom & Maura Foley O'Connell
Killowen, Cork Road, Kenmare
County Kerry
✆ **+353 (0) 64-41013**
🖰 **www.shelburnelodge.com**

Shelburne belongs in the chicest style magazines, for Maura Foley's expert eye makes everything perfect.

Shelburne Lodge is the most tactile of places. Everywhere you look, it seems as if an art director has arranged everything you see, and the art director has been thinking about textures, a tonal palette that changes over the course of the day, the impact of a big canvas, the impact of a small canvas, the heat of the fire, the feel of a fabric, the aroma of cooking.

Other places are styled, but Maura Foley's astoundingly rigorous eye for detail means that Shelburne seems as if it has been art directed, all for maximum effect, but never to a point of overload. Everything syncs here, everything joins together, from the comfort of the sitting room to the tactility of the bedrooms and bathrooms to the amazingly exuberant feast that is breakfast.

Mrs Foley famously ran Packie's restaurant in town, and the precision of the professional chef is seen here, applied in all its attentive glory, to the most important meal of the day – whiskey cream on the porridge; strawberries and pineapple with ginger syrup; the most vividly technicolour poached peaches you ever saw and ate. Fantastic.

- ● **OPEN:** Mar-mid Dec
- ● **ROOMS:** Seven rooms, all en suite
- ● **PRICE:** €110-€165 per room. Single €80-€100

- ● **NOTES:** 🖃Visa, Mastercard, Laser.
No restaurant (good restaurants locally). Enclosed car parking. No ♿ access. Low season special rates available. Children welcome, high chair, cot.

- ● **DIRECTIONS:**
300m from the centre of Kenmare, across from the golf course on the Cork road.

ZUNI

Paul & Paula Byrne
26 Patrick Street, Kilkenny
County Kilkenny
☏ **+353 (0) 56-772 3999**
🖰 **www.zuni.ie**

Classy style that wears its age with impeccable grace makes Zuni the hot Kilkenny destination.

Zuni has been blessed with a great sense of style right from when it first opened, and the proof of the success of that style is that, in the seven years since it was created, it hasn't aged a jot.

Open the doors into the restaurant, into the bar, or into your room, and that classy, confident, cool, calm style makes you feel right at home: dark wood, strong primary colours, simple clean lines in the bathroom. Turning up here one Sunday evening after a long day's work and a long drive, it only took seconds for the style and its confident panache to refresh us, and to make us eager for dinner.

Dinner was great, service was extra attentive, the wine list is markedly improved, and the totality of Zuni was at perfect pitch. As a restaurant with rooms, Zuni makes perfect, consummate sense – the rooms work, the restaurant works, it all works, and it all works very smoothly indeed. Kilkenny had just won the All Ireland that Sunday, and we definitely felt we were in the champion place, in the champion hurling county.

- **OPEN:** All year, except Christmas
- **ROOMS:** 13 rooms, all en suite
- **PRICE:** €50-€90 per person sharing

- **NOTES:** 🖃Visa, Access, Amex, Laser.
Restaurant open for dinner Mon-Sun. ♿ access.
Enclosed private parking at rear.
Children welcome.

- **DIRECTIONS:**
Located in the city centre, on Patrick Street, which is round the corner from Kilkenny Castle. Take M50 from Dublin airport. Take N7 southbound direct to Kilkenny.

IVYLEIGH HOUSE

Dinah & Jerry Campion
Bank Place, Portlaoise
County Laois
✆ **+353 (0) 57-862 2081**
🖰 **www.ivyleigh.com**

Cashel Blue pancakes for breakfast, now isn't that just the thing? Such original details are just one element of Dinah Campion's smart townhouse.

You build great B&B's detail by detail. Here are some of Dinah Campion's details in the lovely Ivyleigh. Plump Frette towels. Gilchrist & Soames toiletries. Sumptuous antique beds. Beautifully restored period details. Extraordinary – unbelievably extraordinary – housekeeping everywhere you look.

And then there's breakfast: poached plums; prunes and apricots; granola; muesli; melon and orange; Cashel Blue pancakes with mushrooms and tomatoes; fresh white bread; fresh brown bread; tea in a glistening silver pot.

Dinah Campion's smart town house, close to the centre of Portlaoise, is a special place, thanks to the endless efforts of the hostess to make it special. Mrs Campion's eye for detail is rigorous, almost ruthless. Everything she can do to make something special, she will do it. And the rub is that she will do it better than anyone. She is a driven person, a meticulous creator of comfort. Merely reciting the breakfast ingredients can't do justice to the originality and intricacy of her cooking, for those Cashel Blue breakfast pancakes are truly special. A brilliant address.

- ● **OPEN:** All year, except Christmas
- ● **ROOMS:** Four rooms, all en suite
- ● **PRICE:** B&B €130 per room. Single room €80

- ● **NOTES:** 💳Visa, Mastercard. No dinner.
No ♿ access.
On street car parking.
Children over 8 years welcome.

- ● **DIRECTIONS:**
In Portlaoise, follow the sign for multi-storey car park. At car park entrance there is a sign with directions for Ivyleigh House.

ROUNDWOOD HOUSE

Frank & Rosemary Kennan
Mountrath
County Laois
✆ **+353 (0) 57-873 2120**
🖰 **www.roundwoodhouse.com**

If you feel it is time you discovered the undiscovered Slieve Bloom region, then let Roundwood House be your base for exploring the Irish pastoral.

Frank and Rosemary Kennan's house makes critics redundant. How do you analyse a lovely Palladian house, set in the heart of the country, which enraptures everyone who stays here. Do you analyse the rapture? The mesmerising impact of the house and hospitality on the guests from all over the globe who find themselves here? Man, you don't analyse rapture – you just feel it. And if you aren't mesmerised by this house, then you are already dead.

But, so as not to feel completely redundant, let's say that the secret of Roundwood, we reckon, is also the secret of the Slieve Bloom area, where Roundwood resides: it's the Irish pastoral at its most profound and, especially if you encounter it for the first time, it is truly striking, elemental, mesmerising. Stay here for a few days and you will feel you have discovered a new region of Ireland. Slieve Bloom is a well-kept secret, and it's an elixir.

And having discovered it, you head back to Roundwood, and Frank's chat and craic, and Rosemary's wonderful cooking, just seem to amplify that perfect pastoral, and to not merely amplify it, but also to encapsulate it.

● **OPEN:** All year, except Christmas & 2-31 Jan
● **ROOMS:** 10 rooms, all with private bathrooms
● **PRICE:** €75-€85 per person sharing. Single supplement €25

● **NOTES:** 🖻All major cards accepted. Dinner, 8pm, €50, communal table. Book by noon. No ♿ access. Children welcome, high chair, cot, babysitting.

● **DIRECTIONS:**
Turn right at traffic lights in Mountrath for Ballyfin, then left onto R440. Travel for 5km on the R440 until you come to the house.

THE COURTHOUSE

Piero & Sandra Melis
Main Street, Kinlough
County Leitrim
℗ **+353 (0) 71-984 2391**
🖱 **www.thecourthouserest.com**

Cucina casalingua, in a nice restaurant with nice roms in nice little Kinlough in quiet little Leitrim, is just the ticket for us, thanks very much indeed.

When we first wrote about Piero Melis's happy little restaurant with rooms in lovely little Kinlough, we compared its civility and culture and completeness with the less happy sprawl of nearby Bundoran, suggesting the latter could learn a lot from the former.

And guess what? We got an offended letter from a member of staff in the local tourism set-up, pointing out what eejits we were, and how we didn't know what on earth we were talking about, and how Bundoran was, actually, a high-class mecca.

So, can we suggest that when you are next in the area, that you stay in Piero's, enjoy his lovely cooking – some home-made ravioli, some smoked swordfish, some john dory with crab sauce, along with some of the super Sardinian wines that he imports. And after a fine breakfast next morning, drive the short distance to Bundoran and assess the place for yourself. Tell us which one you think is a good advertisement for Irish tourism, which place is sustainable, sympathetic, creative and classy. And which is not sustainable, sympathetic, creative or classy.

● **OPEN:** All year except Xmas & two weeks in Nov & Feb
● **ROOMS:** Four rooms
● **PRICE:** B&B €37 per person sharing, €42 single

● **NOTES:** 💳Visa, Mastercard, Laser. ♿ access. Children welcome, but not in the restaurant after 8pm. Dinner 6.30pm-9.30pm, ('till 10pm high summer), €40.

● **DIRECTIONS:**
On the main street in Kinlough, turn off the main Donegal/Sligo road at Bundoran, on the bridge opposite the post office.

HOLLYWELL COUNTRY HOUSE

Rosaleen & Tom Maher
Liberty Hill, Carrick-on-Shannon
County Leitrim
✆ **+353 (0) 71-962 1124**
✉ **hollywell@esatbiz.com**

The Maher family are one of the great hospitality dynasties of modern Ireland, with both parents and sons running superb enterprises.

The Maher family are one of the great dynasties of Irish hospitality. They began by running the local hotel in Carrick, before crossing over the river to run Hollywell. But today the boys are back in town, as Tom and Rosaleen Maher's boys, Conor and Ronan, have made an enormous success of The Oarsman pub in the centre of the town.

To see these chaps at work, to see the care they lavish on their customers and their cooking, is to see a family gene that has hospitality stamped all over it: they are peas from the pod of a family who personify all the good things of hospitality: civility, hard work, respect, true service, a desire to please, a striving for excellence.

And they learnt it all from their folks, who run what is one of the loveliest addresses in the North West. Hollywell is pretty, dignified, companionable, because it is simply so expertly run by the Mahers. It's a cosy house, extremely relaxing, it has delicious cooking, and there is nothing about this area that the Mahers do not know. Above all, they know the art and business of hospitality, for it is written in the bone, and flows in the blood.

● **OPEN:** 1 Mar-31 Oct
● **ROOMS:** Four rooms, all en suite
● **PRICE:** €55-€70 per person sharing. Single supplement €20-€30

● **NOTES:** 🖃All major cards accepted. No dinner. Enclosed car park. No ♿ access.
Children over 12 years welcome.

● **DIRECTIONS:**
From Carrick-on-Shannon, cross the bridge, keep left at Gings pub. The entrance to Hollywell is on the left.

THE MUSTARD SEED

Daniel Mullane
Echo Lodge, Ballingarry
County Limerick
☎ **+353 (0) 69-68508**
🖰 **www.mustardseed.ie**

A great boss and a great
crew contribute to the success of The Mustard Seed,
Dan Mullane's fab house.

Whatever Dan Mullane does, he does it to the very best
of his considerable ability, and he does so to the accom-
paniment of great success.

For ten years he ran the Mustard Seed, in Adare, with
great success and acclaim, before moving his restaurant
here to a beautiful house which now has no fewer than
sixteen glamorous, luxurious rooms. And for more than
ten years now he has enjoyed great success in Echo
Lodge, running one of the great Irish country house
hotels and restaurants.

How does he do it? Simple. He looks after people. He
provides comfort and comforting food. He knows what
you want better than you know yourself. In that regard,
he is the quintessential host. But, what Mr Mullane also
enjoys is the ability to create the perfect space in which
people really enjoy themselves, and the sound of people
enjoying themselves is very much the soundtrack to Mr
Mullane's success. Echo Lodge is a rocking busy restaurant and country house, and its attractions are almost
addictive: given a taste, you immediately crave more.

● **OPEN:** All year, except first two weeks in Feb
● **ROOMS:** 16 rooms, including three suites
● **PRICE:** €90-€160 per person sharing. Single supple-
ment €20-€40, triple room supplement €60

● **NOTES:** 💳Visa, Mastercard, Access.
Dinner €59. ♿ access.
House not suitable for young children.
Pets by arrangement only.

● **DIRECTIONS:**
Take the Killarney road from Adare, 500m until you
reach first turning off to the left, signed for Ballingarry.

GHAN HOUSE

Paul Carroll
Carlingford
County Louth
℡ **+353 (0) 42-937 3682**
🖰 **www.ghanhouse.com**

One of the benchmark addresses of
the border counties, Ghan House is a
perfect retreat for leisure and pleasure
and excellent food in Carlingford.

Paul Carroll has made Ghan House into both the star of
County Louth, and the star of enigmatic little Carlingford.
He has created a benchmark address that manages,
somehow, to keep on getting better and better. Standards
march ever upwards in Ghan House.

His fame has spread most recently into Northern Ireland,
from where the house now pulls in droves of happy travellers and eaters to enjoy the comfort of the rooms, the
food and the wines, the welcome and the charm of the
village. Mr Carroll's house works because he is such an
excellent motivator of his staff, and such a wise student
of the art of hospitality. He is a quiet man, but he has a
steely resolve to do everything to the best of his ability.
His team matches him every step of the way. Nothing is
too much trouble, nothing is too much work.

Even with a rash of new building, much of it out of scale
and unsympathetic, Ghan House remains blessed to be
just on the fringe of Carlingford, one of the most attrac-
tive, quirky, fun villages in the country, and one of the best
weekend destinations to escape to for some r'n'r.

- **OPEN:** All year, except Christmas & New Year
- **ROOMS:** 12 bedrooms, all en suite
- **PRICE:** €95-€100 per person sharing, single from €70

- **NOTES:** 💳Visa, Mastercard, Access, Amex.
Restaurant open Fri-Sat, 7pm-9.30pm. Midweek & Sun
by arrangement, €49.50. No ♿ access.
Children welcome.

- **DIRECTIONS:**
Approaching from south, Ghan House is 1st driveway
on left after 50kph sign on entering Carlingford. 85km
from Dublin, 69km from Belfast.

PARK INN MULRANNY

Tom & Kathleen O'Keefe
Mulranny, Westport
Co Mayo
℡ **+353 (0) 98-36 000**
🖱 **www.mulranny.parkinn.ie**

One of the most brilliant newcomers in years, PIM is set to be one of the major west coast destinations.

Something new

The Park Inn is going to be a major west coast player over the next decade. That's not just because of Seamus Commons' superb cooking – though that alone is reason enough to travel west. Mr Commons cooks glorious food which is served in a glorious dining room, and does so at great value for money.

But it is all the other stuff that is going to make PIM a player. The rooms are gorgeous – one look at the bridal suite and you'll book the reception there and then. The apartments are stunning, beautifully fitted out, really groovy in style, and they made us feel sorry for those poor folk queuing up at airports to get to grotty apartments in Spain and Portugal. Spain and Portugal when you can chill out here, with a blue flag beach just across the road and the promise of dinner later? Holidaying at home suddenly seemed the best invention ever. Having tried PIM at high summer, we would love to try it in autumn, and then in winter, and maybe even a Xmas or New Year break, walking the beaches, driving through Achill, letting that sullen Mayo magic into your blood. Utterly ace.

● **OPEN:** All year, except closed 24th-26th Dec
● **ROOMS:** 41 rooms & 19 apartment suites
● **PRICE:** B&B from €75.00-€105.00 per person sharing. 2 bedroom Apartment Suites mid week €200.00-weekend €260.00

● **NOTES:** 💳Visa, Mastercard, Laser.
Restaurant opens breakfast, lunch & dinner, Dinner €39. Full ♿ access. Private car parking. Children welcome.

● **DIRECTIONS:**
On the N59 just outside Newport and overlooking the sea at Mulranny.

NEWPORT HOUSE

Kieran & Thelma Thompson
Newport
County Mayo
℡ **+353 (0) 98-41222**
🖱 **www.newporthouse.ie**

The most Edwardian, and the most elemental, of the Irish country houses, Newport is gloriously grand.

Newport is one of the most elemental of Irish country houses. It's famed as a destination for fishermen – and indeed even owns its own river, the Newport – but there is a lot more to it than that, just as there is a lot more to it than the fact that Grace Kelly – aka Princess Grace of Monaco – once stayed here, aeons ago, an event trotted out by every writer who visits here.

No, what is most important about Newport is the elemental quality of the house, the cooking, the hospitality. There is an ageless grace about all of these things, and the way they are done here. The style of cooking and service, indeed the style of the entire house, has something almost Edwardian about it. Staying here can feel like stepping into the past, walking through the mystical wardrobe to be confronted by John Betjeman, say, or even J.M. Barrie. But if it is formal, it is not at all frumpy, thanks to a funky little bar – one of our favourites – and to the rich, traditional cooking of the kitchen, a style of food that transcends fashion, especially with the richest eggs Benedict you ever did eat. But, you're worth it.

● **OPEN:** 19 Mar-8 Oct
● **ROOMS:** 18 rooms, 16 en suite
● **PRICE:** B&B €108-€162, Single supplement €22, superior room supplement €26. Dinner B&B €166-€221

● **NOTES:** 💳Visa, Mastercard, Access, Amex.
Restaurant open for casual lunch and formal dinner.
Dinner €60. Limited ♿ access. Children welcome, no charge under 2 yrs, 30% reduction under 12 yrs, sharing. Pets in courtyard rooms.

● **DIRECTIONS:**
In the centre of the village of Newport, on N59 route.

STELLA MARIS

Frances Kelly & Terence McSweeney
Ballycastle
County Mayo
✆ **+353 (0) 96-43322**
🖰 **www.StellaMarisIreland.com**

Frances and Terence's SM is not just one of the stars of the county, it is one of the stars of the entire country.

There was an enormous leatherback turtle washed up on the beach near to Stella Maris when we stayed during the sultry heat wave of July.

It was a pretty exceptional happening – and the McKenna kids got suitably excited and got their cameras out – but for the adults, it seemed to be another example of the exceptionalism that is the currency of Ballycastle.

There are all the wonderful painters who come here to work, for example – the magical Stuart Shils is our poster boy – and the excellent Munnelly's tea rooms and Polke's pub, and the astonishing Céide Fields just up the road. And there is Stella Maris, Frances Kelly and Terence McNally's brilliant country house hotel.

Stella is a true star. It's demure in style, and the cooking at dinner and breakfast is amongst the very finest in the entire country. Everything the five McKennas ate at both meals was pitch perfect – perfect dinner, perfect breakfast, perfect everything and, amidst all the perfection, there was a tiramisu that was nothing other than magic. Star of the sea? Stella Maris is star of the country!

● **OPEN:** Easter-early Oct
● **ROOMS:** 11 rooms
● **PRICE:** B&B €100-€125 per person sharing

● **NOTES:** 📷Visa, Mastercard, Access.
♿ access. Limited ability to accommodate young children. Dinner 7pm-9pm (until 10pm weekends), €40.

● **DIRECTIONS:**
Go down the hill from Ballycastle, and the Stella Maris is signposted from here. Turn right, it's on the Pier Road, overlooking the sea.

WESTPORT PLAZA HOTEL

John Clesham
Castlebar Street, Westport
County Mayo
℡ +353 (0) 98-51166
🖰 www.westportplazahotel.ie

A hugely promising new venture in handsome Westport, the Plaza has a warm style all of its own.

Something new

Newport has been developing like crazy over the last several years, with the pretty town adding new hotels and houses like crazy. And yet, the town has yet to build the sort of strong hospitality profile of a town like Kenmare or Kinsale – to date it hasn't offered up the small handful of champions needed to attract media attention and to create signature destinations – though there is some very fine cooking in The Lemon Peel, should you be wondering where to have dinner.

But The Plaza shows signs of being the sort of development that could be the start of something interesting. This sister hotel to the nearby Castlecourt Hotel gets the basic things right: the meeting and greeting by local staff is first rate, all the front-of-house team are excellent, the beds and bedrooms are first class – check out those big mattresses – and the place is comfortable, funky, good value, with lots of strong warm colours, cosy nooks to relax in, and some excellent food coming from the kitchen. The value and the service will definitely bring people back, and this is the start of something good.

● **OPEN:** All year
● **ROOMS:** Seven rooms, all en suite
● **PRICE:** B&B €60-€115 per person sharing, single supplement €35

● **NOTES:** 🖃All major credit cards accepted.
Restaurant Merlot opens for breakfast and dinner, dinner €36.50. Plaza bar food all day.
Full ♿ access. Private free car parking.
Children welcome.

● **DIRECTIONS:**
In the centre of Westport, on the N5 from Castlebar.

CASTLE LESLIE

Sammy Leslie
Glaslough
County Monaghan
✆ **+353 (0) 47-88100**
🖱 **www.castleleslie.com**

A small universe all on its own, with a breathless scheme of developments, Castle Leslie nevertheless remains one of the most magical country houses.

Castle Leslie is fast becoming a world all on its own, with a new cookery school under the control of head chef Noel McMeel, new bedrooms completed, with a series of new houses being built on part of the estate grounds, with equestrianism and fishing and everything else you could think of, all happening at ferocious pace of development under the vigilant and more-than-capable eye of Sammy Leslie. If Rick Sten can transform Padstow in Padstein, Sammy Leslie seems determined to transform Glaslough into Leslielough.

All of this extraneous stuff is a little bit beyond our remit in the modest Bridgestone Guides. So let's just say that Noel McMeel is one of the masterly modern Irish chefs, and his cooking is alive and well and in pristine form in CL. The rooms in the house are gothic and almost obscenely gargantuan, and everyone loves them to bits. Castle Leslie is such a vast panjandrum that staying here feels like taking part in a fairy tale, a feeling which perhaps explains why it is a favourite place for so many visitors. There is absolutely nowhere else quite like Castle Leslie.

● **OPEN:** all year, including Christmas
● **ROOMS:** 20 rooms
● **PRICE:** All inclusive price of €500 per person per night – includes dinner, B&B

● **NOTES:** 🔲 Visa, Mastercard, Amex. No ♿ access. No children under 18 years. Communal Dinner served 8pm. Cookery school. Hunting Lodge hotel open 2007, children welcome in Lodge.

● **DIRECTIONS:**
2 hours from Dublin off the N2. Detailed directions can be found on their website.

WHIGSBOROUGH HOUSE

Anna Heagney
Fivealley, Birr
Co Offaly
© **+353 (0) 57-9133318**
🖰 **whigsborough@eircom.net**

What a lovely country house escape Whigsborough is, thanks to Anna's charm, and excellent cooking.

Something new

Anna Heagney is a fine cook, and her graceful, flavourful, light country house cookery is the perfect grace note for graceful, charming Whigsborough House, a fine old pile, part of which dates from the 1740's, which sits amidst the eskers of Fivealley, a few miles north of Birr in County Offaly.

Part of the house's charm is the fact that it is not rabidly new-fangled, design-driven and colour magazine trendy. It's a slow, stately, small manor house, and Anna − who rented the house and took guests years back before she bought the house − runs it with smiling affability and calm. And with a lot of culinary skill. You choose from the month's menu a couple of days in advance, allowing the kitchen the chance to make sure everything works. Tomato, saffron, ricotta and olive tart shows the sort of imagination at work here, whilst elderflower marinated chicken with a salad of aubergine and roasted pepper is right on the money. Meringue mess does just what it says, a panjandrum of sticky sweetness. Lovely food, lovely host, lovely, lovely house.

● **OPEN:** All year, except Christmas
● **ROOMS:** Three double rooms & one single room
● **PRICE:** B&B €40-€50 per person sharing, €40-€50 single

● **NOTES:** 💳No credit cards.
Dinner available, €37-€42. Advance booking essential, and you are requested to order in advance.
No ♿ access. Private car parking. Children welcome.

● **DIRECTIONS:**
From Birr the N52 for Tullamore to Fivealley, left for Banagher, immediately left, house 1 km on right.

KINGSFORT COUNTRY HOUSE

**Corine Ledanois &
Bernard Eucher-Lahon
Ballintogher, County Sligo**
℅ **+353 (0) 71-9115111**
🖱 **www.kingsfortcountryhouse.com**

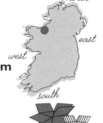

A beautiful piece of
Francophone style in
County Sligo, Kingsfort is a
very stylish newcomer.

A slice of Provençal style, in deepest Sligo, Kingsfort is an amazing sport of nature. When we arrived, the sun was dappling through the trees, the driveway threw up dry south-western dust as the car wheels drove over the tiny pebbles, a couple were sitting at a steel garden table in the courtyard drinking a bottle of red wine, and the white and pale green colouring and the artfully confected brico-lage style all had us asking a simple question: did we just bilocate to Southern France? Where are the vineyards?

Well, no, we hadn't shifted countries. We had just arrived at one of the chicest new destinations in the north west, a glorious piece of design that has what it needs to be one of the major new players.

There is one double family room and one other bedroom in the house, and 6 rooms outside in the courtyard. The dining room is small, and doubles as the breakfast room. Breakfast was very fine, and local breads from Brid Torrades' bakery are a smart touch. Yeatsian scholars who want to get as close as possible to Lough Gill will want to stay here, close to that mellow, magic water.

- **OPEN:** All year, except Christmas
- **ROOMS:** Eight rooms, all en suite
- **PRICE:** B&B €40-€80 per person sharing, €15-€20 single supplement

- **NOTES:** 💳Visa, Master, Amex. Dinner available, €40. ♿ access. Private car parking. Children welcome. Enquire about special rates. Mobile tel no: 087-2467292.

- **DIRECTIONS:**
Leave the main Dublin/Sligo road at the Collooney roundabout. Travel in the direction of Dromahair. At Ballygawley you will find signs for the house.

GREAT BREAKFASTS

1

BALLYMALOE HOUSE
SHANAGARRY, Co CORK

2

COXTOWN MANOR
LAGHEY, Co DONEGAL

3

DEVON DELL
GALWAY, Co GALWAY

4

GLASHA FARMHOUSE
BALLYMACARBRY, Co WATERFORD

5

GLEBE SHORE
SKIBBEREEN, Co CORK

6

GORTNADIHA LODGE
RING, Co WATERFORD

7

HANORA'S COTTAGE
NIRE VALLEY, Co WATERFORD

8

LONGUEVILLE HOUSE
MALLOW, Co CORK

9

MONART
ENNISCORTHY, Co WEXFORD

10

THE OLD CONVENT
CLOGHEEN, Co WATERFORD

INCH HOUSE

John & Nora Egan
Thurles
County Tipperary
© **+353 (0) 504-51261/51348**
🖰 **www.inchhouse.ie**

Natural, elemental generosity is the
heartbeat of the Egan family's Inch
House, and do look out for those little
crucifixes above the bedroom doors.

If there is a signature element to Inch House, a symbol
and a signifier that remains with you after you have left
this fine old pile in the heart of Tipperary, it is the sheer
generosity of the entire crew who run this fine big manor
house just a few miles from Thurles. Everything about
Inch is generous, so much so they should rename it: Inch?
Huh, it's a Mile at any rate.

The rooms are generous in size and very comfortable –
and if we mention again the little crucifix above the door
of each room it may give you some insight into the unaf-
fected way in which the Egan family run their house. The
cooking from Kieran O'Dwyer, who has run the kitchens
here since 1996, is a deliciously generous country cooking that makes the restaurant the destination address for
miles around: smoked salmon tagliatelle; chicken wrapped
in bacon and stuffed with garlic and herbs; entrecote with
cracked black pepper – and the dining room is a superbly
comfortable, elegant space, both for dinner and breakfast.
Put all of the elements together and you understand why
Inch is such a local hero, a most generous local hero.

- ● **OPEN:** All year, except Christmas
- ● **ROOMS:** Five rooms, all en suite
- ● **PRICE:** €58 per person sharing, Single €68

- ● **NOTES:** 🖃 Visa, Master, Laser, Dinner 7pm-9.30pm
Tue-Sat, €45-€47. No ♿ access.
Children welcome, early dinner for under eight years,
who are not permitted in dining room after 7pm.

- ● **DIRECTIONS:**
6.4km from Thurles on the Nenagh road.
Turn off at the Turnpike on the main N8 road, signpost
Thurles.

THE OLD CONVENT

Dermot & Christine Gannon
Clogheen
County Tipperary
✆ **+353 (0) 52-65565**
🖰 **www.theoldconvent.ie**

Something new

Salvation for food lovers
lies just outside Clogheen,
in Dermot and Christine's
fantastic The Old Convent.

'The house found us', is how Christine Gannon describes discovering and deciding to set up shop in the fine old building that is The Old Convent, just on the edge of Clogheen, in the heart of the Golden Vale. Given that Mrs Gannon hails all the way from Colorado, and Mr Gannon from Clifden in Connemara, the house was an expert seeker of the right talent. And that the Gannons are the right talent to run this 'Gourmet Hideaway', with its lovely dining room and seven fantastic bedrooms, can be in no doubt. Right from the outset, the only difficulty with TOC was getting a table or getting a room.

The rooms are beautifully realised, shimmering with colour yet pared down, showing the influence of Mr Gannon's mentor, Paddy Foyle of The Quay House. Big plump beds, lush baths and cosy rooms are further warmed by the embrace of the louring hills just behind the house: this is a special place, with a special atmosphere. As one would expect, breakfasts are pitch perfect, dinner is a sumptuous feast of pitch perfect tastes, and that's simply what The Old Convent is: pitch perfect.

- **OPEN:** All year, except Christmas & annual holiday
- **ROOMS:** Seven rooms, all en suite
- **PRICE:** B&B €60-€80 per person sharing, €25 single supplement

- **NOTES:** 💳Visa, Master, Laser.
Dinner in restaurant, 8-course tasting menu, €50.
No ♿ access. Private car parking.
Children over 12 years welcome.

- **DIRECTIONS:**
The Old Convent is located on the R668 Cahir to Lismore road.

AN BOHREEN

Jim & Ann Mulligan
Killineen West, Dungarvan
County Waterford
℡ +353 (0) 51-291010
🖳 www.anbohreen.com

The Mulligans' An Bohreen is a B&B with a difference, with a professional polish thanks to Ann Mulligan's truly fine, modern country cooking.

'We recently stayed at An Bohreen near Dungarven (sic) and couldn't agree more with your recommendation. B&B's are always hit and miss affairs but we couldn't fault the whole experience with Jim and Ann'.

That is pretty much the standard reaction we receive here at Bridgestone central about An Bohreen, and have received since they first opened their doors. Jim and Ann Mulligan put together an irresistible mix of great cooking, superb hospitality and a lovely aesthetic and, when you add in some fantastic value for money, you really do have something special, a B&B which really over-delivers on every front.

For us, it is the utterly rigorous attention Ann devotes to every detail of everything you eat in An Bohreen – from the roast Waterford lamb at dinner to the potato cake with a generous Irish breakfast – that singles out this pretty house. This is not the domestic cooking you expect in a B&B: instead it is a professionally delivered masterclass in serious cuisine, and it is the icing on the cake of a pretty bumper destination.

- **OPEN:** 5 May-29 Oct
- **ROOMS:** Four rooms
- **PRICE:** €40-€45 per person sharing. Single €55-€60

- **NOTES:** 📷Visa, Mastercard, Laser. Dinner 6.30pm-8pm, €37, book by noon. No ♿ access. Secure parking. No children under 12 years.

- **DIRECTIONS:**
Coming from Waterford on the N25, after the town of Lemybrien, look for the resume speed sign. 5km later there is a right turn, travel 220m and you will see a sign for the house.

GLASHA FARMHOUSE

Olive O'Gorman
Ballymacarbry
County Waterford
© +353 (0) 52-36108
🖰 www.glashafarmhouse.com

Athletic walkers and hikers are amongst the devotees of Olive Gorman's bumper breakfasts and good country comfortable cooking.

It takes about two paragraphs of print just to list all of the wonderful things Olive O'Gorman presents and parades for breakfast every morning in Glasha. Every manner of fruit is here, every manner of bread, every manner of egg dish, every manner of cereal, every manner of drink. If you are a serious walker, then this cornucopia may present a dilemma. If you are an amateur rambler like us, then it's simply a pure delight.

This is one of the very best breakfasts you can encounter in Ireland and, for the walkers in the Knockmealdown and Comeragh Mountains, which many of the guests in Glasha are, it is the very thing to put a spring in your step as you set off to hike up a hill or two in the rain.

And, when you get back, soaked, exhausted, worn out, wind-blown, then there are comfortable rooms with all the necessary kit, and a comfortable, nicely domestic dinner cooked with great care by Olive to look forward to, friendly food, consoling cooking, that is just what you feel like eating after a hard day's tramp over the mountains. And, tomorrow, let's do the whole thing over again.

- **OPEN:** all year, except Christmas
- **ROOMS:** Eight rooms, all en suite
- **PRICE:** B&B €100-€120 per room.
Single rate €50-€60

- **NOTES:** 💳Visa, Mastercard.
Dinner 7pm-8pm €25-€35, BYO wine.
Children over 12 years welcome. Secure parking.
♿ access.

- **DIRECTIONS:**
Well signposted, off the R671 between Clonmel and Dungarvan. 3km from Ballymacarbry.

GORTNADIHA LODGE

Eileen & Tom Harty
Ring, Dungarvan
County Waterford
℡ **+353 (0) 58-46142**
🖰 **waterfordfarms.com/gortnadiha**

Eileen Harty is renowned as one of the great hostesses, but she deserves more renown as creator of one of the most amazing breakfasts in Ireland.

We have friends, seriously critical food lovers, the sort of people who won't leave the house unless they know exactly where they are eating for every meal of any planned trip. You know these guys: they are people who, when eating lunch, will be discussing what they will be going to have for dinner. You know these people. They have standards, and the fundamental standard is that life is too short to ever have an indifferent meal. Not even a bad meal, but an indifferent meal. Far, far too short. Perish the thought. God forbid.

Anyway, these friends, should you care to ask them, will tell you that the best – the best – breakfast they have ever eaten in Ireland was prepared by Eileen Harty at Gortnadiha. What did they eat? Everything. You name it, you enumerate it, and it was there to be enjoyed. How long did it last? Hours. Literally: a two hour breakfast, can you credit that? Anything your heart could desire, and Mrs Harty had it prepared. And prepared to perfection. Dickensian generosity. Blissville for breakfast. And one of the great hostesses to chat to, an unforgettable event.

● **OPEN:** 1 Feb-1 Dec
● **ROOMS:** Three rooms, all en suite
● **PRICE:** €40-€50 per person sharing, €10 single supplement

● **NOTES:** 🖻Visa, Mastercard. No dinner. No ♿ access. Children welcome. Visa, Private parking.

● **DIRECTIONS:**
Follow the curve of Dungarvan Bay. Come off the N25 at the junction for Ring (3km west of Dungarvan). Signposted from here. Midway between Waterford and Cork. 2 hours from Rosslare.

HANORA'S COTTAGE

Mary Wall
Nire Valley, Ballymacarbry
County Waterford
☏ **+353 (0) 52-36134**
🖰 **www.hanorascottage.com**

Mary Wall over-delivers on every detail of her famous breakfast, not least her signature muesli, one of the great bowls of breakfast healthfulness.

We have written elsewhere in this book about the wonderful porridge prepared by Eunice Power in another great County Waterford address, Powersfield House, in Dungarvan.

But long before Mrs Power was stirring the oats, Mary Wall was concocting one of the great health foods in Hanora's Cottage, up in the hills of Ballymacarbry. For one of the absolutely unmissable elements of Mrs Wall's astonishing breakfasts is her signature muesli, which contains bran, pinhead oatmeal, jumbo oats and lots and lots of dried fruits, all stirred together into one of the great bowls of breakfast health.

And that is symbolic of how Mary Wall works. She tweaks and twists things to get them her way, whether it is with the rooms in Hanora's, or with her signature breakfast, or her signature muesli. Her application makes for a clamorously comfortable place to stay, to spend a few days walking the hills, working off the gargantuan breakfast that you enjoy every morning, and with a good dinner cooked by Eoin Wall to look forward to at day's end.

● **OPEN:** All year, except Christmas (open New Year)
● **ROOMS:** 10 rooms
● **PRICE:** €85-€125 per person sharing.
Single room €85

● **NOTES:** 💳Visa, Mastercard.
Restaurant open 6.30pm-9pm.
No ♿ access. No facilities for children under 12 years.
Secure parking. Special offers off season.

● **DIRECTIONS:**
From Clonmel or Dungarvan, follow signs to
Ballymacarbry. The house is signposted from the bridge.

PARKSWOOD HOUSE

Roger & Terrie Pooley
Passage East
Co Waterford
✆ **+353 (0) 51-380863**
🖱 **www.parkswood.com**

Parkswood is a hugely promising newcomer, with a spectacular elevated site and an air of quiet comfort.

Roger and Terrie Pooley's lovely house above Passage East enjoys the most spectacular site, high above the Waterford Estuary, with views ever onwards towards Cheekpoint and Dunbrody Abbey. There is a new conservatory added to the house, and welcoming tables on the lawn, where afternoon tea or a glass of wine can be enjoyed.

The Pooleys are great hosts, great to chat to, up-to-speed on whatever information you might need, and very friendly, and Parkswood House itself is just big enough to have presence, but not at all grand. There are five bedrooms and some have little balconies and double doors that open out to take in the view. There's also a separate self-catering cottage/bungalow in the grounds with its own entrance.

So far, so brilliant, and after such a short time in business Parkswood is a truly promising destination. A little more variety at breakfast time, and a little more luxuriousness with toiletries and bedclothes, will just bring all the pleasure-filled potential of this fine house into sharper focus.

- **OPEN:** All year, except Christmas
- **ROOMS:** Four rooms, all en suite
- **PRICE:** €60 per person sharing. Single supplement €10

- **NOTES:** 🚫No credit cards.
Dinner available given notice. Children welcome.
♿ access from 2007. Self-catering cottage available.
Discounts for long stay.

- **DIRECTIONS:**
R683 from Waterford for 3 miles then take the R684 to Passage East. Located 3 miles along on the left-hand side.

POWERSFIELD HOUSE

Eunice & Edmund Power
Ballinamuck West, Dungarvan
County Waterford
℅ **+353 (0) 58-45594**
🖰 **www.powersfield.com**

You seek not merely the greatest bowl of porridge, but also a cure for the nation's ills? You will find it in Powersfield, believe us you will.

Eunice Power is one of those mighty women who, irrespective of what they do, simply has to do it the best.

Take, for instance, the porridge which Mrs Power prepares for breakfast in the lovely little dining room of Powersfield House.

Into the mellifluous mix of oatmeal she adds linseeds, sesame seeds, sunflower seeds, and raisins. It's a mixture that, put together, could sustain the fate of nations. If Ireland went to work on a breakfast of Mrs Power's Porridge, the Celtic Tiger would quickly succeed America as the leading superpower, schoolchildren would have Mensa-grade IQs, and the country would be, finally, settled. Mrs Power's porridge is oatmeal as elixir, as superfood, as rocket fuel for the body. The future health of the nation resides here, in a bowl at breakfastime. And everything else is just as fine as the porridge.

And she achieves this by simply asking: how do I do this the best way? That's the question she asks about every detail of Powersfield, and that's why it is such a special, distinctive and individual house.

● **OPEN:** All year, except Christmas, open New Year
● **ROOMS:** Five rooms, all en suite
● **PRICE:** €55-€60 per person sharing. Single room €65-€75

● **NOTES:** 🖃Amex, Visa, Mastercard, Laser.
Dinner for guests only, €27-€35.
Full ♿ access.
Children welcome.

● **DIRECTIONS:**
Follow Clonmel road from Dungarvan, the house is the second turn to the left, and the first house on the right.

RICHMOND HOUSE

Paul & Claire Deevy
Cappoquin
County Waterford
℡ **+353 (0) 58-54278**
🖱 **www.richmondhouse.net**

Graceful and understated excellence, and Richmond also possesses the friendliest staff in the country.

How to describe Richmond House? It is wonderful, friendly, timeless, elegant and ever so slightly frayed around the edges, which gives the house tremendous character.

How to describe the people who run it? Paul Deevy is one of the most low-key and self-effacing chefs you will ever meet. His wife, Claire, is a gracious and sincere host who sometimes seems to doubt that the food her husband and his crew cook can really be as good as people insist it is. But it is that good, it really is.

How to describe the people who look after you? As we noted above, the staff are the friendliest you can find. They mollycoddle you, because they know that you do, deep down, want to be mollycoddled.

How to describe what you experience at Richmond? Well, we think it is hospitality at its purest, and hospitality at its most natural. Hospitality that flows instinctively, hospitality that is found in the greeting, the cooking and serving, the leave-taking. There is nowhere else quite like this charming country house. Richmond is sui generis.

● **OPEN:** 20 Jan-20 Dec
● **ROOMS:** Nine rooms
● **PRICE:** from €75 per person sharing, Single supplement €20

● **NOTES:** 💳All major cards accepted.
Restaurant open for dinner only, Mon-Sun (closed on Sun in winter), €50.
Private parking.
Children welcome, babysitting, toys.

● **DIRECTIONS:**
Just outside Cappoquin, the house is well signposted.

THE TANNERY TOWNHOUSE

Paul & Máire Flynn
10 Quay Street, Dungarvan
County Waterford
✆ **+353 (0) 58-45420**
🖱 **www.tannery.ie**

*Both the Townhouse and
the Tannery are benchmark,
special occasion destina-
tions, as good as it gets.*

We have a friend who got engaged during the course of an evening having dinner in The Tannery, and staying in The Tannery Townhouse. That is a mark of the sort of feel-good, special-occasion, darling-will-you-be-mine sort of place that Paul and Máire Flynn have created. It is a mark, also, of how The Tannery has now become more than just a restaurant with rooms, a modern, swish d'n'd – dinner and duvet. It's a destination address. It's a special occasion place. It's snipes of champagne and asking the question and red carpet dressing and sleeping late and all that good stuff we need in our lives.

How did Paul and Máire do it? The same way everyone else does it – hard work, talent, and going out on a limb. When the restaurant opened, it was so far ahead of its time it took locals ages to realise what a jewel it was. When the Townhouse opened, they too pushed the envelope, offering a hyper-stylish new concept that proved to be the most romantic thing you can get your hands on. Both ventures, now beloved, were bold steps at the time. But then fortune favours the brave. So, go on, ask her...

● **OPEN:** All year, except Christmas
● **ROOMS:** Seven rooms, all en suite
● **PRICE:** from €60 per person sharing, Single €70, superior rooms €160

● **NOTES:** 💳All major cards accepted. Tannery Restaurant is open for lunch and dinner, €45-€50. Two private parking spaces (otherwise street parking).

● **DIRECTIONS:**
20m from The Tannery Restaurant, at the end of Main Street, which is just down from the main square, beside the Old Market House building.

10 PLACES WITH

GREAT STYLE

1

THE CLARENCE
DUBLIN, Co DUBLIN

2

THE G
GALWAY Co GALWAY

3

GLEBE SHORE
SKIBBEREEN, Co CORK

4

KINGSFORT COUNTRY HOUSE
BALLINTOGHER, Co SLIGO

5

MARLAGH LODGE
BALLYMENA, Co ANTRIM

6

MONART
ENNISCORTHY, Co WEXFORD

7

THE OLD CONVENT
CLOGHEEN, Co WATERFORD

8

THE ROSS
KILLARNEY, Co KERRY

9

SHELBURNE LODGE
KENMARE, Co KERRY

10

TANNERY TOWNHOUSE
DUNGARVAN, Co WATERFORD

TEMPLE

Declan & Bernadette Fagan
Horseleap, Moate,
Co Westmeath
+353 (0) 57-933 5118
www.templespa.ie

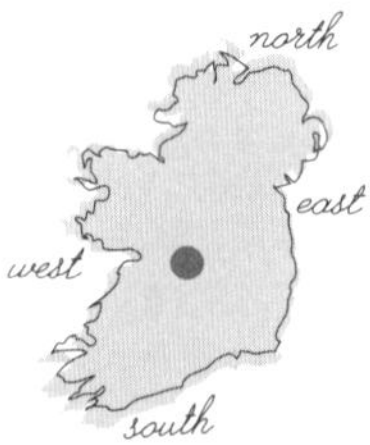

Temple is the smartest hotel and spa development, and deserves to win each and every award there is.

We have railed against the rash of 4-star hotels that now litter the country, those tax-break mausoleums 'as personable as airport lounges' as one wise food lover once remarked.

So, how would we have done things? Simple, we would have mandated Bernadette and Declan Fagan's new Temple as the exemplar of all future hotel development. Twenty rooms, beautifully integrated into its landscape, forming a continuum with the house where they began B&B and with the spa they built several years back. Temple deserves to win awards for architecture, for conservation, for staff excellence, for spa excellence, for food excellence. It is an icon in every way: individual, gifted with its own signature style, with the owners having managed the difficult task of retaining the ambience that graced the old Temple house. Temple is testament to two remarkable people, and their remarkable vision of a genuinely holistic environment for people to relax and to find peace and focus. Declan and Bernadette are true stars, and Temple is proof of their philosophy, and their importance.

- **OPEN:** All year, except Christmas
- **ROOMS:** 23 rooms, all en suite
- **PRICE:** All inclusive rates: 24 hour escape €245 p.p.s. for 24hrs midweek, Single €265.Spa Weekends from €435 p.p.s. Fri-Sun, €475 single.

- **NOTES:** Visa, Mastercard, Access, Amex. Dinner, 8pm. Inclusive rates only. ♿ access.
Children over 16 years only.

- **DIRECTIONS:**
1km off the N6 Dublin-Galway road, and clearly signposted just after Horseleap, heading westwards.

WINEPORT LODGE

Jane English & Ray Byrne
Glassan, Athlone
County Westmeath
℡ **+353 (0) 90-643 9010**
www.wineport.ie

As addictive as pink champagne or Bill Charlap playing Leonard Bernstein, Wineport is a Midlands star.

Let the magic of Wineport Lodge sink into your veins, indulge too much in the heavenly location, the lovely cooking, the astoundingly fine service, and you will find it hard to leave this idyllic lakeside hideaway, and to drag yourself back to the real world.

Ray Byrne and Jane English have crated something distinctly magical here, on the shores of Lough Ree. They are pioneering folk, and they are masters of the art and practice of hospitality, and masters of carrying it out in their own quiet way. They have allowed Wineport to evolve organically from its original incarnation as a restaurant into this sympathetic and astute complex, which now has more than twenty bedrooms along with the restaurant and various meeting rooms. Their patience in developing Wineport means that it sits in its jaw-droppingly beautiful environs snugly, appositely, whilst inside the attention to detail from the entire crew – and this crew has been working together for a long time now – is simply second-to-none. But, a warning: Wineport is as addictive as any classy narcotic, so practice moderation. In moderation.

- ● **OPEN:** All year
- ● **ROOMS:** 29 rooms
- ● **PRICE:** B&B €165-€395 per double room. Weekend breaks also.

- ● **NOTES:** ▆All major cards accepted.
Restaurant serves dinner, à la carte menu approx €55.
♿ access.

- ● **DIRECTIONS:**
At Athlone, take the Longford exit off Dublin/Galway rd, fork left at the Dog & Duck, Lodge is 1.5km further on on the left.

BALLINKEELE HOUSE

John & Margaret Maher
Enniscorthy
County Wexford
© **+353 (0) 53-913 8105**
🖰 **www.ballinkeele.com**

A perfect base for exploring Wexford and discovering its fine opera festival, Ballinkeele is one of those fine country houses where everything is just right.

Sky-high standards, and impeccable attention to detail, are the keynotes of John and Margaret Maher's fine country house, close to Enniscorthy. The Mahers are expert at making everything sync together – the food is local and agrestic in flavour, the country house cooking you were hoping to enjoy as you drove down the N11 to the house. The rooms are magnificently maintained, with just the right period detail observed. But where other country house rooms can seem cold or dull, these are colourful and feel special, luxurious, elegant. The dining room and public rooms are grand, capacious, never overbearing. Behind all this pleasing effect lies that attention to detail that makes Ballinkeele work, yet the Mahers don't act like professional hospitality folk: they simply have that professionalism, but they express it in a very shy, understated, utterly charming way.

It is this that makes the house so winning, and which makes you feel so comfortable. Opera buffs should note that they stay open until the end of the Wexford opera festival, so your opera base is ready and waiting for you.

- **OPEN:** Open Feb-end Oct
- **ROOMS:** five double rooms, all en suite
- **PRICE:** €70-€90 per person sharing,
Single supplement €20

- **NOTES:** 🖃All major cards accepted. Dinner €40, please book by 11.30am. Children welcome, but no under 12s allowed in dining room at dinner. No ♿ access.

- **DIRECTIONS:**
From Wexford, take the N11, and the house is signposted on your right.

115

KELLY'S RESORT HOTEL

Bill Kelly
Rosslare
County Wexford
☏ **+353 (0) 53-913 2114**
🖰 **www.kellys.ie**

Bill Kelly should be made Ireland's Tsar for happiness, such is the volume of blissfulness he creates.

'Did get to spend a week in Kelly's and had the most wonderful time – just fantastic'. So says Orla Broderick, echoing so many of the family visitors to Bill Kelly's great shrine to hospitality in Ireland's sunny south-east.

In the fifteen years or so that we have been making the pilgrimage to the shrine of Kelly's, as the kids have gotten older and their needs and wants have changed, two things have stood out about the Kelly's experience. Firstly, this hotel is constantly striving to improve, and succeeding in so doing. Better rooms, better design, better aesthetic. Secondly, as the kids' needs have changed, so the hotel proves adept at letting them do what they want. They progress from the children's tea to the dining room, from organised games to swimming and sports with others. And for the adults? Well, we just want to bask in that ambrosia of great food, great art works, the chill-out ambience that is congratulated by their superb spa, and the amazing new rooms. We want to feel part of that happy family of regulars for whom Kelly's promises and delivers 'the most wonderful time – just fantastic'.

● **OPEN:** Late Feb-early Dec
● **ROOMS:** 120 rooms, all en suite
● **PRICE:** Spring/autumn: weekend rate €315pp + 10% service charge; 5-day midweek from €590pp + 10% service charge. Summer: 7-day rate from €915pp + 10%

● **NOTES:** 💳All major cards accepted. All rates include full board. La Marine restaurant also comes recommended. ♿ access. Every facility for babies and children.

● **DIRECTIONS:**
Clearly signposted in Rosslare and from the main Wexford-Rosslare Harbour road.

MONART

Amanda Corrigan
The Still, Enniscorthy
Co Wexford
℡ +353 (0) 53-923 0999
🖰 www.monart.ie

Monart is our sort of spa: a temple to good health that also managed to serve the very best dessert of the year.

Something new

Discreet yet impressive, luxurious yet restrained, Monart is the most significant new arrival on the Irish hospitality scene in many a year. Part of the brilliant design reminds us of New York's Guggenheim, with winding, sloping walk-ways and concourses taking you between the spa itself and the main body of the hotel. Arranged around the lake, the bedroom and restaurant wings curve organically, and the money spent, and the care and attention paid, is all evident, but not in any sort of egotistical manner. Others have built temples to excess, but Liam Griffin has simply built a fine temple.

The cooking is as mature and fully-formed as everything else – mushoom consommé with chanterelle tortellini; home-cured salmon; pork belly with red cabbage and prune jus, healthful food that shines with goodness. And, as nothing is as healthful as being happy, Monart made the best pudding of the year, a trembling white chocolate and Kahlua soufflé with a jug of crème anglaise and vanilla ice cream. High rollers will love the wine list. Great break-fasts, great staff, and an all-round stellar achievement.

- **OPEN:** All year, except Christmas
- **ROOMS:** 70 rooms
- **PRICE:** €135-€235 per person sharing, €195 upgrade for suite, single supplement €30

- **NOTES:** 💳All major cards accepted. Dinner, €60. ♿ access. Adults (over 18) only. Spa open 8am-9pm. No functions. D, B&B rates quoted, see website for these and other special offers.

- **DIRECTIONS:**
Just off the N11 road to Gorey, there is a very good downloadable map on their website.

SALVILLE HOUSE

Jane & Gordon Parker
Salville, Enniscorthy
County Wexford
℃ **+353 (0) 53-923 5252**
🖰 **www.salvillehouse.com**

With lovely food, lovely
style and design, lovely hospitality, Salville is the house
that simply has it all.

In recent years, when writing this book, we have tended
to focus on Gordon Parker's cooking as being the USP of
Salville House.

Well, fair enough, actually, for this man is one of our
favourite cooks, with a style of food so pure, svelte and
personal that dinner in Salville is always, effortlessly,
amongst the finest country house cooking in Ireland.
Amateur eagerness meets professional polish in this
man's kitchen. But focusing on the cooking means that we
perhaps neglect the style and character of the house
itself, and that is a mistake, because this is a simply peachy
country house, and the Parkers have a style of decorating
and designing which is vivid, personal and delightful. We
have noted before that the effect of staying here is to be
utterly uplifted, because with each element in the right
place – style, food, company, location – you feel that
everything you are experiencing when you stay here, and
eat here, has the vivid reality of a painting, a painting
which you just happen to be a part of. A tableau vivant,
with you at the centre, having the best time imaginable.

● **OPEN:** All year, except Christmas
● **ROOMS:** Five rooms. One two-bedroom self-con-
tained apartment available for B&B or self catering
● **PRICE:** €45-€50 per person sharing

● **NOTES:** No credit cards.
Dinner, 8pm, €35. Book 24 hours in advance.
No ঙ access. Secure parking.

● **DIRECTIONS:**
Leaving Enniscorthy on the N11 to Wexford, take the
first left after the hospital, go up the hill to a T-junction
then turn left and proceed for 500m

BALLYKNOCKEN HOUSE

Catherine Fulvio
Glenealy, Ashford
County Wicklow
☎ +353 (0) 404-44627
🖰 www.ballyknocken.com

Catherine Fulvio is not just amazingly accomplished, she is amazingly accomplished at a very young age. Honestly! Young people today!

In a couple of years time, when people talk about the singular contribution made to Ireland's food and hospitality cultures by the great female chefs and hostesses of the country, have no doubt that Catherine Fulvio's name will be amongst them.

Myrtle, Maura, Darina, Bernadette, Giana, Merrie, Adele, on and on will go the list of distinguished women, and Catherine of Ballyknocken House will be there too, flying the flag for the new generation of women.

For Mrs Fulvio is not merely accomplished, she is super-accomplished, and all at a very young age. She runs a beautiful house, she operates a hugely successful small cookery school, and she has a young family to look after all at the same time. And, then, when you might happen to turn up at a meeting to discuss tourism or contemporary Irish food, Mrs Fulvio will be there also, her contributions always apposite, modest and witty. She is a renaissance woman, and her beautiful house and its lovely food is the finest proof of her accomplishment. If you want to see a star in the ascendent, Ballyknocken is for you.

● **OPEN:** Feb-Nov
● **ROOMS:** Seven rooms
● **PRICE:** From €59-€65 per person sharing. Single supplement €35

● **NOTES:** 💳Visa, Mastercard. Dinner, Tue-Sat, €38. No ♿ access. Children welcome. Cookery school. Short break rates online.

● **DIRECTIONS:**
From Dublin, head south to Ashford (on N11), then turn right after Chester Beatty pub. Continue for 5km and the house is on the right.

THE BROOK LODGE INN

Evan, Eoin & Bernard Doyle
Macreddin Village, Aughrim
County Wicklow
✆ **+353 (0) 402-36444**
🖰 **www.brooklodge.com**

If you could bottle the confidence coursing through the Brook Lodge right now, you would have some wild elixir.

Evan Doyle and his crew in The Brook Lodge are on some sort of mighty roll right now. We have never seen this imaginative and original address exude such confidence, such panache, such a sense of power. The confidence of the staff is totally winning, the kitchen is producing the best food the kitchen has ever produced, and it all adds up to a mighty concoction.

How to explain the success? It's easy: the Brook Lodge espouses an organic, sustainable style in everything it does and, like any serious destination, it has thereby taken its time to find its rhythm, to find its signature, to hone its style, to become itself. Evan Doyle is quite the wisest of proprietors and, like any wise man, he is in no hurry, he is not in a rush. He knows that everything happens in its time and, precisely because of that, everything then happens in the right time. In the hectic Ireland of today, such patience is extra-valuable, and it also explains why the Brook Lodge is such a vital retreat for folk from the big city: The Brook Lodge talks it, and walks it. It is sustainable, patient, calm, and altogether pretty darn magnificent.

● **OPEN:** All year, including Christmas
● **ROOMS:** 66 rooms and suites
● **PRICE:** €115-€130 per person sharing, single supplement €40.

● **NOTES:** 🖳All major cards accepted. Restaurant, pubs, market and bakery, dinner €60. Secure car parking. Reservations essential. Limited ♿ access.
Children welcome. Check web rates for B&B & Dinner.

● **DIRECTIONS:**
N11 to Rathnew. Right at r'about, to Glenealy, on to Rathdrum. 1.5km outside Rathdrum, right towards Aughrim.

ANNA'S HOUSE

Anna Johnson
Tullynagee, 35 Lisbarnett Rd
Comber, County Down
© **+44 (0) 28-9754 1566**
⌂ **www.annashouse.com**

Travellers from all over the
world aren't the only visitors
to Anna's: professionals
come here to see a true cult.

Anna Johnson's house is the sort of house that other
people in the hospitality industry will stay at when visit-
ing County Down.

After all, every serious student of the business wants to
see how a master of the art does it. And, so, pilgrimages
by professionals are made to Comber, to see how you
run a superb house, cook superb food, plan and master a
superb garden.

For that is what Anna, and Ken, do here in Anna's House.
It's close to the big city, but it feels like it's in another
country, such is the perfect illusion of away-from-it-all
that the house creates. But that is only one element of
the magic. The cooking for both breakfast and dinner is a
fabulous style of true country cooking that you might
have believed had all but disappeared: it hasn't, and if you
want to reconnect with it, with tastes from your child-
hood, then it is here for you.

Above all, staying at Anna's gives the feeling that you have
found a new home. You feel you belong here, no matter
where you are from. That is some achievement.

● **OPEN:** All year, except Christmas
● **ROOMS:** Three rooms
● **PRICE:** £70-£80 per double room, £45 single room

● **NOTES:** ▭No credit cards accepted. No dinner.
Secure car parking. ♿ access. Babies welcome, not suitable for children (because of lake). Internet access.

● **DIRECTIONS:**
In Lisbane pass the petrol station, turn right into
Lisbarnett Road. After 1km & after a right-hand bend
follow a private concrete lane leading up the hill.

THE CARRIAGE HOUSE

Maureen Griffith
71 Main Street, Dundrum
County Down
℡ +44 (0) 28-4375 1635
🖰 **www.carriagehousedundrum.com**

Maureen Griffith is one of the
pioneers of hospitality in Northern
Ireland, and her lovely house is one of
the jewels of fast-moving Dundrum.

With new restaurants and seafood bars opening,
Dundrum is on its way to being the Kinsale or Kenmare
of County Down. And when it gets there, it will be important to remember Maureen Griffith as one of the great
pioneers of hospitality in the village.

Mrs Griffith ran the ever-splendid Buck's Head Inn, before
moving sideways into The Carriage House. As such, she
has presided over two great establishments, bringing to
both her splendid style with design and with food. That
sense of style is particularly important, for it means the
three rooms in the house all have the most apposite,
youthful, colourful style, with flowers and treat-filled trays
and plump pillows on plump beds beckoning you to lay
down and close tired eyelids on tired eyes.

In the morning, there is an excellent organic breakfast on
offer, along with great fruit salads and compotes, fresh
breads, yet another treat in a house that feels like a suc-
cession of treats. And, don't forget your bike, for Mrs
Griffiths even has a place to store that safely. So remember, in years to come, Maureen Griffith was here first.

- **OPEN:** All year
- **ROOMS:** Three rooms, all en suite
- **PRICE:** £60 double room, Single room £40

- **NOTES:** 📷 Visa, Mastercard.
No dinner, but excellent restaurant, The Buck's Head,
just next door. Children welcome. Storage for guests
travelling on bicycles. No ♿ access.

- **DIRECTIONS:**
Dundrum is on the main Belfast to Newcastle road
(A24), and The Carriage House is in the centre of town.

THE INN AT CASTLEDAWSON

Simon Toye & Kathy Tully
47 Main Street, Castledawson
County Londonderry
✆ **+44 (0) 48-7946 9777**
🖰 **www.theinnatcastledawson.co.uk**

Castledawson is going to become one of the great food hubs in Northern Ireland, with Simon and Kathy's Inn right at the heart of everything.

Simon and Kathy are an ambitious, professional pair, and The Inn in quiet little Castledawson is just the right venue for this talented team to write their reputation over the coming years.

Good, large scale bedrooms mean that the best way to enjoy The Inn is to take a night away from home, enjoy the drive, then settle down for an excellent dinner cooked by Mr Toye. His modern, unshowy style is what you would expect from someone who learnt his skills working alongside Belfast's most distinguished restaurateur, Nick Price. Like his mentor, Mr Toye's cooking reads straightforward – prawn and monkfish brochette; sirloin with tobacco onions; chicken with potato, pancetta and cabbage gratin; rare-breed pork with apricot stuffing; egg custard tart – but there is a subtlety and flair here that is very winning, making this some of the very best cooking in the North.

Ms Tully, meantime, runs everything with confident panache, easily on top of her game. There is great promise here, and great promise has been already realised.

- **OPEN:** All year, except New Year's Day and 26th Dec
- **ROOMS:** 12 rooms
- **PRICE:** £35-£40 for double room, £50 single room

- **NOTES:** 🖃 Mastercard, Visa, Switch, Maestro.
Restaurant open lunch & dinner.
♿ access.
Secure parking for 12 cars.
Children welcome, children's menu. Under 15s £10.

- **DIRECTIONS:**
On the main street, just down from the church.

GREAT ROMANCE

1

BALLYVOLANE
CASTLELYONS, Co CORK

2

THE BROOK LODGE INN
MACREDDIN, Co WICKLOW

3

CASTLE LESLIE
GLASLOUGH, Co MONAGHAN

4

CUCINA
KINSALE, Co CORK

5

THE G
GALWAY, Co GALWAY

6

KILGRANEY HOUSE
BAGENALSTOWN, Co CARLOW

7

THE MERCHANT
BELFAST, NORTHERN IRELAND

8

THE MORRISON
DUBLIN, Co DUBLIN

9

THE ROSS
KILLARNEY, Co KILLARNEY

10

TANNERY TOWNHOUSE
DUNGARVAN, Co WATERFORD

MALMAISON

Mark Davies
34-38 Victoria Street, Belfast
BT1 3GH
✆ **+44 (0) 28-902 20200**
🖱 **www.malmaison.com**

The Malmaison style may be overdone in the bar, but dining rooms and bedrooms in the Mal are super.

Malmaison hotels are witty. Beside the toiletries in your bathroom, for instance, a note says: 'Take me'.

'Lap me up' reads the milk bottle shaped door hang, asking to deliver a quarter pint of milk to your door. It's amusing and irreverent, this playfulness, and it fits in with the slightly baroque design of the hotel, which is angular, jokey, tongue-in-cheek, and yet appositely correct.

We like the dining room and the more restrained style of the bedrooms in the hotel, but the bar is an eyesore and really should be worked on straight away – this room doesn't know what it wants to be. Whilst the dining room is pleasingly murky at evening time, it feels a little dark at breakfast, due to an absence of natural light, but the busy staff and the fine attention to detail seen in the buffet table, and in a correctly prepared breakfast of poached egg with hollandaise on a muffin with field mushrooms serve to concentrate the mind.

The staff are engaging but, for Belfast, somewhat uncharacteristically restrained – they should relax a bit more and make sure the wit isn't just on the funny signage.

- **OPEN:** All year
- **ROOMS:** 64 rooms, all en suite
- **PRICE:** £99-£160 per room

- **NOTES:** 💳Visa, Master, Amex.
Brasserie open breakfast, lunch & dinner.
♿ access. promotionalrates available, see web for details
No private car parking.
Children welcome.

- **DIRECTIONS:** On the right-hand side of the street as you approach the Albert Clock in Belfast's city centre.

MARLAGH LODGE

Robert & Rachel Thompson
71 Moorfields Road, Ballymena
County Antrim
℡ **+44 (0) 28-2563 1505**
⌂ **www.marlaghlodge.com**

Read on to discover this
year's adjectives to describe
the skills of Robert and
Rachel Thompson.

In this era of information overload, it takes some nerve
to run a guest house where the rooms have neither tel-
evision, nor music system. Robert and Rachel Thompson
have that nerve. None of Marlagh's three beautiful rooms
have any techie stuff. Hooray!

Actually, Robert and Rachel not only have nerve, they
have great taste. Marlagh is a beautiful house, which this
most creative couple have meticulously and painstakingly
restored. But then, that is the word to describe this pair:
painstaking. And there is another adjective that fits, too:
autodidactic. Give them a task, present them with a chal-
lenge, and they will master everything they turn their
hand to: decorating and design, cooking and wine appre-
ciation, hospitality and service.

They are a formidable pair, and a mighty team, and
Marlagh, with its pitch-perfect style and Rachel's fabulous
cooking – Mrs Thompson cooks some of the best food in
the North – is testament to the intertwining of two truly
great talents, people whose painstaking autodidacticism
makes for the most singular, satisfying aesthetic.

● **OPEN:** Open all year
● **ROOMS:** Three rooms, all en suite
● **PRICE:** B&B £80 per room, £40 single

● **NOTES:**
▦ Mastercard, Visa, Switch, Maestro.
Dinner, 8pm (book by noon), £32
No ♿ access.
Children welcome.

● **DIRECTIONS:**
From the A36 to Larne, turn onto Rankinstown Road,
and the driveway is immediately on your left.

THE MERCHANT

**Adrian McLaughlin
35-39 Waring Street
Cathedral Quarter, Belfast
℡ +44 (0) 28-9023 4888
🖥 www.themerchanthotel.com**

Grand style comes to
Belfast, and The Merchant
over-delivers on the detail,
while giving good value.

Something new

You get a good, firm handshake when you check in at The Merchant, a simple, direct gesture that has all but vanished from other establishments, and which many new hotels – which The Merchant is – wouldn't have the sense to realise is so important.

It's a sign that The Merchant is trying hard, trying to have signature gestures and a signature style, something they need in order to justify their high prices. Wisely, they have maintained the character of this fine old Ulster Bank building, both in the public rooms and in the bedrooms, leaving idiosyncrasies such as not-quite-straight walls, to considerable effect. Of course, the plasma screen tv is here, and the American wrap-around bed, but they fit well amidst the ornateness of the rooms, and the rooms are blessedly quiet. The staff over-deliver when it comes to making restaurant reservations and organising transport in their cars around town, delivering that feeling of being luxuriously swaddled. Breakfast is served in the very grand dining room and is very well executed. The Merchant is an fine totality, and is actually good value.

- **OPEN:** All year, except Christmas
- **ROOMS:** 26 rooms
- **PRICE:** B&B £220 per room

- **NOTES:** 💳All major cards accepted.
Dinner in restaurant, £40-£50.
♿ access.
Children welcome.

- **DIRECTIONS:**
Belfast city centre, near the River Lagan. A map can be downloaded from their website.

PAUL ARTHURS

Paul Arthurs
66 Main Street, Kircubbin
County Down
℡ **+44 (0) 28-4273 8192**
🖰 **www.paul/arthurs.com**

Paul Arthurs' flavour-filled cooking is a real treat that makes the drive down the peninsula to Kircubbin a journey packed with ravenous promise.

Paul Arthurs' progress through the maze of modern Irish food and hospitality has been patient, wise, and hugely successful. He was born into the world of food, coming from a family of butchers, and his instinct and respect for food has always been pre-eminent in his work. This man understands food and cooking in a profound way, and he does things his own way.

He has a restaurant with rooms and a chipper in Kircubbin, and the rooms have meant that making a big night out, and taking a drive down the peninsula to enjoy his cooking, is a cinch. The rooms are comfortable and well appointed, with good linens and towels, just what you would expect from the modern dinner 'n' duvet arrangement, and value for money is keen.

This allows everyone to focus on some truly fine modern Irish cooking from this dynamic one-man-band, with fish and shellfish dripping with lemony, garlicky flavours, with ace sirloin of beef packed with grassy, herbaceous scents and a lovely Café de Paris butter, then, nice, simple puddings to send you off up the stairs, as happy as Larry.

● **OPEN:** Open all year, except Jan
● **ROOMS:** Seven rooms, all en suite
● **PRICE:**£70 per double room, sharing. Single room £50. £10 supplement for children sharing room.

● **NOTES:**
Visa, Mastercard.
Dinner in Paul Arthurs' restaurant, £28.
Stair lift for disabled.

● **DIRECTIONS:**
Right in the middle of main street in the village, on the left-hand side as you drive towards Portaferry.

INDEX

The Bridgestone Food Lover's Guide To Northern Ireland

ISBN 1-874076-75-8

'Quite simply, indispensable'. *The Irish News*

'These little books pack quite a punch', *The Irish Times*

Irish Food

Slow & Traditional
ISBN 1-874076-68-85

Fast & Modern
with Paul Flynn
ISBN 1-874076-67-7

Irish Seafood Cookery

with Martin Shanahan

ISBN 1-874076-77-4

'Sixty great recipes',
The Irish Times

'I highly recommend this book', Ed Behr, *The Art o Eating*, (on *How to Run a Restaurant*)

How to Run a Restaurar

ISBN 1-874076-55-3

How to Succeed in Hospitality

ISBN 1-874076-56-1

by John McKenna

New Titles

The Bridgestone 100 Restaurants in Ireland 2007

published November 06

ISBN 1-874076-80-4

The companion volume to this guide.

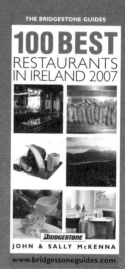

The Bridgestone Irish Food Guide

published Spring 2007

ISBN 978-1-874076-84-7

'A fantastically comprehensive guide to eating in Ireland', *The Sunday Independent*, (on the last edition)

KEEP IN TOUCH WITH WHAT'S HAPPENING IN
IRISH FOOD

www.bridgestoneguides.com

publishes regular updates to entries listed in the
Bridgestone Guides, as well as links to hundreds of
good web addresses in Irish Food.

There is also an on-line service for buying books.

Sign up for our website newsletter Megabytes, and we'll
be sure to keep you posted.